INVESTING IN V

Inside the Strategies, Tactics and Routines of World-class Watch Investors and Supercollectors

----

Oliver Simon

Disclaimer

This book is designed to provide information that the author believes to be accurate on the subject matter it covers, but it is sold with the understanding that neither the author nor the publisher is offering individualized advice tailored to any specific portfolio or to any individual's particular needs, or rendering investment advice or other professional services such as legal or accounting advice. A competent professional's services should be sought if one needs expert assistance in areas that include investment, legal and accounting advice. This publication references data collected over many time periods. Past results do not guarantee future returns. Additionally, performance or return data, in addition to laws and regulations, change over time, which could change the status of the information in this book. This book solely provides historical data to discuss and illustrate the underlying principles. Additionally, this book is not intended to serve as the basis for any financial decision; as a recommendation of a specific investment advisor; or as an offer to sell or purchase any security or watch. No warranty is made with respect to the accuracy or completeness of the information contained herein, and both the author and the publisher specifically disclaim any responsibility for any liability, loss or risk, personal or otherwise, which is incurred as a consequence, directly or indirectly, of the use and application of any of the contents of this book. In the text that follows, many people's names and identifying characteristics might have been changed.

Table of Content

If you were looking for lost empires here tomorrow

you'd wear a Rolex

When a man's life depends on his watch, the chances are he wears a Rolex.

It's a big, tough, working watch.

The Oyster case is carved out of a solid block of hardened Swedish stainless steel or gold. And safe inside those solid walls is a 26-jewel self-winding officially certified Swiss chronometer.

Because so much of the work is done by hand it takes us more than a year to build a Rolex.

The men, who have been risking their lives diving for archaeological treasure in the Yucatan*, feel it was time well spent.

The Rolex they wear is the Submariner, individually tested and guaranteed to a depth of 660 feet, provided case, crown and crystal are intact. $225.00 with matching bracelet.

*Photographed at the sacrificial well in Chichen Itza for Expeditions Unlimited, Inc.

Official Timepiece, Pan American World Airways

ROLEX

AMERICAN ROLEX WATCH CORPORATION, 580 FIFTH AVENUE, NEW YORK, N.Y. 10036.
Also available in Canada. Write for free color catalog.

6

Foreword

An Investment on Your Wrist

S uccessful investing is never easy. Investing in watches is no exception. Whoever thinks the contrary does not know what he is talking about. Competition is fierce, and many market participants in this tightly knit community turn out to be extremely savvy professionals in their field. Many former watch collectors who turned investors in this lucrative and intellectually rewarding playing field can count on years of experience with this asset class. Yet, it is one of the most worthwhile investment disciplines, if you really want to master it.

Put differently, investing in watches combines the fierceness of the stock market with even higher barriers to entry but, in turn, also imperfect information and less competition from passive or computer-driven investors. At the top end of the high-profile auction range your competition for returns are wealthy entrepreneurs and family dynasties. At the lower end you encounter executives, fund managers, doctors and entrepreneurs who compete against you. In short, this game attracts some of the smartest individuals on the planet who also have the financial means and passion for playing it properly. However, different from the stock market, not everybody who is buying or selling in the watch world is a financially motivated investor. Passion-driven collectors and casual consumers give the watch market a unique spin and make it so imperfect yet rewarding. Whether you bring previous experience from your first watch investments or you are just starting out, you need to be well prepared before committing capital to this niche. This book helps you with this task and shall be your first steppingstone. Despite the incredible popularity of wristwatches as collectibles and the vast sums of money involved, there are very few resources for watch enthusiasts that even make an attempt to approach the subject from an investment angle. Hence, it is the goal of this book to level the playing field for you and explain the basic dynamics of the watch game. This is done in a fast, approachable, and straightforward way—at roughly the same price as a Frappuccino in Geneva.

In stark contrast to typical museum-quality, high-gloss books aimed at collectors and advanced investors with a penchant for great photography and dramatic presentation that can cost as much as the service for an entry-level vintage watch, this book represents an affordable introduction into the topic in an analytical yet practical way—no matter whether you are a complete newcomer or you have already invested in timepieces. Far from being esoteric, this book will help you to take the next step forward. While I hope that all sounds great and exciting, you must be aware of what this book cannot teach you: passion and patience. Investing in watches requires first and foremost time and dedication. Watch prices don't increase over a matter of days, not even months (most of the time); real value appreciation can take much more time than just a couple of years. If you believe in the investment merits of a particular watch, you'll need to be able to hang on to it for a considerable time and withstand any pressure to make a quick flip.

It is therefore of paramount importance to have realistic expectations and the right mindset when you are looking to invest in watches. Be prepared not only to invest money but also a considerable amount of time—time familiarizing yourself with brands, models, and what about specific references or pieces makes them so unique. Only then can the hunt begin. Making a good purchase means finding a watch that will do more to your net worth than just retaining value. Investing in watches means making serious returns. Hence, this guide goes beyond merely discussing auction results; it will teach you to replicate them in the future.

About the Author

The German author, Oliver Simon, is not just a watch aficionado but an expert on the economics of watch investments and ownership. The professional cross-asset investor, who talked already watches with Warren Buffett, bought his first vintage watch, an early Rolex GMT-Master II, at a time when watches were hardly considered an investable asset, but a fast depreciating luxury good—without exception. Over the last two decades, Oliver's interest in vintage and neo-vintage watches has only grown, and his portfolio of investment-grade watches has steadily evolved. It was the special mix of design proportions, mechanical finesse, historical relevance and alternative investment characteristics that pulled the professional investor deeper and deeper into the world of watches. For Oliver, entering into the world of fine timepieces and breaking away from many high-tech consumables and technology gadgets were truly awakening. Especially vintage watches offered him a way to break out of the ephemeral world in which his generation, the early millennials, grew up. A world where every smartphone, smartwatch or tablet only lasts a couple of months or years before it suffers its technical doomsday and becomes obsolete. Much before he considered watches as an emerging asset class, vintage watches became his mechanical, somewhat old school, anchor in an increasingly fast-paced technology-driven world. He is a confessing watch nerd, but an investor by heart. In his debut in the field of horological authorship, Oliver looks back at two decades of expertise in this still somewhat esoteric field, explains the opportunities and challenges that watch investors are facing and gives an accessible primer to the world of watch investing.

Introduction

Why You Should Read This Book

"Time is Money"

– Benjamin Franklin

For watch enthusiasts, a fine timekeeping piece is both a blend of a historical artifact and a symbol of status. As an engineering marvel and a wearable luxury masterpiece, the finest watches of the world are among the most highly coveted objects of desire. For investors seeking sound returns and diversification, however, the underlying financial merits of such *passion assets* can be equally appealing. A watch can be much more than simply a tool for measuring time and expressing style. It can be a piece of legacy AND a sound investment. Passion assets are often referred to as alternative investments, sometimes even as "alternative alternatives". The term, used from everything from vintage cars to hedge funds, is itself some sort of an oxymoron. The word *investment* usually stands for value appreciation while *alternative* suggests turning away from classic concepts and forging a new path. Whatever you precisely want to call them, passion assets, like watches, should also let your inner fire burn. Done rightly, they will then also unfold their financial merits. Studying them, hunting them down, wearing them, and selling them at the right point in time are all steps in the circular process of managing your portfolio. This is what *Investing in Watches* is all about. But let us take a step back for a second. Why should you invest in watches in the first place? In the age of ubiquitous smartphones, smartwatches, activity trackers, and other super-accurate electronic devices, a mechanically powered watch is, in theory, the last needed thing on earth. Who doesn't carry around a smartphone that can tell the time with unmatchable accuracy nowadays? Still, the appeal of a well-manufactured, fine piece of mechanical art has never been higher than today.

"In Switzerland right now, interest rates are minus one, in the UK they're zero, and there's a core group of people out there who rely on yields to have a lifestyle. We have clients who say they'd love to be more involved with the stock market, but with these numbers and P/E ratios, we can't. The bond market's not an option. So they're looking for something else."

– James Marks, Head of Phillips Watches London
& former hedge fund manager (Barber, 2020)

Once a true niche market, watches are now beginning to catch investors' eyes more and more. And this comes with the promise of attractive returns, no matter in which direction stock and bond markets move or the real estate pendulum, gold price or bitcoin swings. Thereby watches are introducing welcome decorrelation effects into more and more investment portfolios. An allocation of fine watches can also serve as an anchor for your personal portfolio. It stabilizes it, not only against helicopter money

11

from global central banks and negative rates but also against bursting bubbles in other financial assets. Consequently, the market for watch investments is today booming at an unprecedented pace. Auctions for vintage watches at major auction houses such as Sotheby's or Christie's keep achieving new all-time records. In 2017, Paul Newman's Rolex Daytona sold for the mind-boggling amount of $17.8 million. Sure, that is rarefied air, but quality vintage watches can already be bought for a few hundred dollars. If you increase that to a few thousand dollars, you can very quickly reach real *investment-grade* terrain with high-quality pieces, even for the likes of Rolex. In particular, the sub $15k market is highly liquid and growing aggressively in recent years. That's still a lot of money, but correctly done, it is well invested, meaning you surely don't have to be a millionaire bidding at high-profile auctions to diversify your wealth with a personal portfolio allocation to watches.

At the time of most of this writing, we were almost a decade into the current stock market bull rally. Recently, the market began to react to the global health crisis caused by the coronavirus. Stock markets sold off more than 30 percent at some point in spring 2020, and also bond markets came under extreme stress and tight liquidity. In such a difficult situation and with central banks printing new money at record speed, it pays off to hold a diversified portfolio of various assets in your personal portfolio and look beyond only paper-wealth. Next to real assets such as real estate or gold, a portfolio of investment-grade watches should be a key part of every diversified inflation-proof wealth portfolio being built. And by reading this book, you are taking the right first step. The watch market is evolving quickly and tends to adjust fast to new information. This primer cannot give you exact recommendations on which watch to buy right now but seeks instead to equip you with the bigger picture and help you to build your own framework to conduct the right investment decisions all by yourself.

Before you get too excited, let me start with an inconvenient truth: the majority of watches, meaning more than 95 percent, are not suitable for investing purposes (no worries, we will define what that term means in great detail later). That doesn't mean at all that they are not desirable in general. Maybe you are wearing one of these pieces right now and love it. They might be amazing pieces in a personal collection of accessories for the modern gentleman or help to celebrate a towering achievement in life. And that is totally fine. However, only the vast minority of watches qualifies as a tangible, alternative asset while the majority has little merit as an investment and instead depreciates over time. The largest part of watches currently in production, the ones you see on your walk to work in high-street boutiques, lack most of the unique characteristics of a sound investment, as I will explain throughout this book. Putting your hard-earned cash into such pieces for any other reason than to enjoy their beauty and mechanical finesse as a luxury *consumption good* is neither logical nor advisable. It would be similar to classifying a brand-new Range Rover or Mercedes S-Class as an investment that you are buying straight from the dealership (hint: except for sporadic cases, it is not—the same holds true for most watches). Instead, a watch investor shall focus on the remaining 5 percent of the watch universe. There is no firm nomenclature for this niche of investment-grade watches. Throughout this book I therefore might call them *collectible, rare* or *fine*. Look at them as synonymously used terms.

Becoming the Insider

To any watch novice acquiring a 15, 20, or 50-year-old watch purely as an investment is everything but straightforward. Doing so needs a specific skill set that every prospective investor first has to build: you first acquire the knowledge; then you acquire the watch. While there are many examples of watches that have increased enormously in value and make it look like an easy ride in hindsight, without proper preparation (or a ton of luck), it is not. The investment process comprises certain steps that can be a delicate matter and that require a similar degree of diligence that a fundamental equity investor would dedicate to his stock selection. It is not by pure chance that James Marks, the new head of auction house Phillips'

London office, is a former hedge fund manager. Now, investing in decades-old mechanical masterpieces surely is not a strategy for investing the majority of your retirement funds. Although you can do very well by keeping a significant portion of your net worth in watches over the years, I urge you to diversify and not put all your eggs into one basket.

Diversification is the only free lunch in investing, so don't say no to it. Depending on your personal circumstances and your profile as an investor, the size of one particular egg and the number of eggs may vary. My default advice is to put a mid-single-digit percentage of your surplus savings or net worth into a portfolio of high-quality classic watches; five percent is usually a good starting point. The underlying economic environment and investment alternatives, as well as interest rates, influence this percentage somewhat. Watches generally serve as a portfolio diversifier and a hedge against market uncertainty, but it is especially in a low or negative interest environment with looming inflation where a non-yielding asset can leverage all its strengths. Similarly to commodities such as gold, watches won't produce an annual yield or interest rate. The investment returns come solely from the appreciation of the asset. At the time of most of this writing, interest rates around the globe have hit the lower bound or are still in negative territory. At the same time inflation worries are becoming more prevalent. This is an environment where you definitely want to have part of your wealth allocated to high-quality real assets such as watches and where that percentage might be even on the higher single-digit side.

This is the new Rolex Chronograph.

Named "Daytona" after the International Speedway where
Rolex is official timepiece.

Its tachometer is engraved on the bezel for easy mph reading.

It has one-minute, 30-minute and 12-hour recorders.

The sweep second hand times to 1/5 of a second.

The 17-jewel movement is enclosed
in a stainless steel waterproof* oyster case.

The Rolex Daytona Chronograph.
With black or white face,
matching stainless steel bracelet.
$210 including Federal tax.

ROLEX

AMERICAN ROLEX WATCH CORP., 580 FIFTH AVE., NEW YORK, N. Y.

* When case, crown and crystal are intact. All prices f. t. i.

15

No Time to Lose

You might be thinking now, how do I—as a watch novice—acquire the kind of expertise to succeed in this field? And if most watches are non-investable, how can I know what the remaining 5 percent of investable timepieces are? Or maybe you are thinking, I'm going to hunt for some classic watches right now. But which brands and which models shall you specifically look out for? What are the key value drivers? And what complications or materials promise the best return on your investment? What are the risks and how can you prepare for them? I can assure you that all of these questions and many more will be answered in this book. *Investing in Watches* shall be nothing less than your ultimate introductory guide in the often complex but always very rewarding and intellectually stimulating world of watch investing.

This primer can't claim to be a comprehensive compendium, as even hundreds of pages would not suffice to properly cover the whole watch investing world. It will nonetheless provide you with the basics to avoid being on the losing end during your quest. If you are an investor at heart and keen to diversify your personal wealth, then this book is the perfect match for you. It will help you to curate a starting portfolio of exceptional timepieces boasting not only immense historical value but also extraordinary investment characteristics and return potential. So let's not waste any further time and jump right into it!

Part I: Why Invest in Watches?

The Big Picture

This book is structured into consecutive five parts. Before jumping right into the core topic of this book, it is necessary to first establish a common understanding of some terms, themes, and definitions that we will use throughout this book. A common starting point helps to better align our thought process during the next few chapters. It will give you the *Big Picture* before we deal in detail with the question of how to invest successfully in vintage (and contemporary) watches and diversify your personal wealth through horological assets.

First of all, we need to manifest that the value of a watch is not simply related to a certain set of technical qualities, complications, or manufacturing finesse. If this were the case, things would be too easy, and you could embark straight on buying a couple of perpetual calendars. In fact, the value of a watch comprises a much larger, however also vaguer, set of value drivers. In other words, just because a watch is built of the most precious materials and boasts a vast set of complications, it will NOT automatically be among the most valuable watches. Sure, it will likely be very precious, but other *less tangible* factors also matter a lot.

We can use the analogy of a floating iceberg to draw a comparison. Icebergs have a significant proportion of their mass below the surface of the seawater. While factors of a watch such as the case material or a rare complication are immediately visible (i.e. are literally the tip of the iceberg), the true value of the watch is determined by a much bigger set of value factors (i.e. the larger piece of the iceberg that is hidden below the water's surface). These include, for example, its previous owner (provenance) or originality (condition). This true fundamental value below the water surface is what watch investing really is all about. In fact, the meticulous analysis successful watch investors conduct is very similar to the research fundamental investors in other disciplines such as real estate or stock picking would conduct.

A good friend of mine and probably one of the best and most diligent watch investors in London always says the following about the required work before actually investing in a timepiece: it is a combination of the work a forensic research analyst would do before investing in the stock of a publicly listed company and the work of a professional art or real estate appraiser. His mind-blowing track record in the world of watches with several home-runs shows me that he is probably right with this.

Similarly to other assets, it is the market that ultimately decides the value of a watch—exclusively and often irrespective of tangible or seemingly objective criteria. If we draw another comparison to the stock market, then the basic characteristics of a watch such as movement, complications, or case material would be components that make up an abstract form of equity book value. However, as with stocks, this book value, i.e. the easily identifiable value parameters, can differ dramatically from the real market

18

value, at least temporarily—like the mass of the iceberg under the surface of the water.

"Without passion, you don't have energy. Without energy, you have nothing."

– Warren Buffett

The essence of this analogy is that the unique presence of a somewhat vague value component, which is often quite challenging to define, makes investing in watches so exciting, so difficult and yet so rewarding. This book will help to deconstruct this dilemma and make watches more accessible as investments for everybody. In contrast to many other traditional asset classes, in the watch world we are still at the very beginning of a growing understanding and interest in its investment merits. There is little doubt that rare timepieces will always remain a niche investment and a non-mainstream asset class. However, I am convinced that their importance will continue to rise dramatically, and the 2020s only mark the very early days of a wave of investor appreciation for the years to come.

Obviously, an expensive mechanical watch is a perfect paradox. It is an anachronism in a time when smartphones tell the time more accurately. Yet, when attending the big auctions in Geneva, I am every time more surprised how this still young asset class is increasingly able to capture the attention of some of the most successful, intelligent, powerful, and skilled investors and businessmen. For most of these individuals investing in watches is a mix of challenge and passion. *Passion* tends to be a term that is sometimes looked down upon by professional investors. Still, in fact, it is one of the most critical ingredients in every professional or analytical discipline. Without passion, you quickly lack the required stamina in your research and due diligence, and you are less likely to go the extra mile. Just look at Warren Buffett. He loves to analyze businesses and their stocks. He wants to understand them in detail, and his day-to-day work is certainly full of passion. Similarly, if you don't have a passion for timepieces, it will not be impossible, but it will definitely become more difficult to invest successfully in them.

A few years ago, I was meeting my friend Antoine for the first time at an Antiquorum auction in Geneva. Antoine is a meanwhile retired French finance entrepreneur and watch enthusiast who turned from casual watch collector to serious investor a couple of years ago. He loved watches ever since and after the great financial crisis of 2008/09 started to put a larger amount of his net worth into alternative real assets. He acquired amongst others a lovely trio of classic British racing cars and, more importantly, built a small but marvelous portfolio of rare Rolex watches. Every time our conversations drifted into investment merits of a certain reference, I could hardly tell whether we were talking about a business or a watch. When he showed me his latest investment timepieces, the analysis was so in-depth that it was easy to see how much work he put into the research—just like he would have done back in the days when he was buying stakes in companies that were in distress. Not everyone in this market will go down such an extreme research route. But the rally in classic watch prices over the last decades only underlines the ever-growing interest in this asset class that lets investors combine their passion for timepieces with a desire for sound, decorrelated returns.

Let us now define classic watches as investments a bit more closely. How can a watch become an asset? And how does a certain decades-old vintage timepiece increase in value and another not? And—one of the hottest and most controversial topics and the question I get asked most—why are classic watches more *investable* than contemporary pieces when ceramic Daytonas and 15202s are trading way above their retail price?

Setting the Scene

What Exactly Is a Classic Watch?

"People want to buy something they cannot buy [...] but if you have money and you buy a watch that other people can buy also, how are you different? [...] But if it is a classic watch [...] you buy exclusivity, you buy individuality, you have something that people don't have."

– Jean-Claude Biver, Head of Watches LVMH & President Hublot
(Barber, 2016)

Aside from *vintage*, the terms *classic*, and (to a lesser extent) *collectible*, and *rare* are used synonymously in his book when discussing investment-grade watches. All of these terms usually describe a precious timepiece for which production has been entirely ceased for either several years or decades and the total number of pieces is finite and often declining. Because of their limited number, their value increases even more as their hands mark the passing of time. Prices for such watches are determined exclusively by demand, with the supply being limited (and often in decline). And as of today, there is no sign of that demand going away anytime soon.

The fundamental idea of collecting watches that are no longer in production did not really appear until the late 1970s and early 1980s. It was less than five decades ago when the emergence of quartz-powered movement technology led the Swiss luxury watch industry to teeter on the brink of collapse. More accurate quartz movements from Japan were suddenly en vogue, and for quite some time it seemed that the end for Swiss manufacturers using mechanical movements had finally arrived. It was this sudden advent of a non-mechanical movement technology that also sparked a brand-new parallel trend: acquiring classic watches as long-term investments. This trend was triggered not overnight but slowly by the reawakening of what was at that time a nearly dead mechanical watch market. Since then, it has become a bigger and bigger movement year over year. In essence, it was the gap between newly emerged quartz watches and the history and craftsmanship of a mechanical piece that was just unsustainably wide and ultimately started reverting throughout the early 1990s. What began initially as a reversion is now reaching a new peak every other year since then. And it is no wonder that until today we see no slow-down in this trend. In today's age of mass-market tailored uniformity, a vintage wristwatch can be an effortlessly eye-catching masterpiece of art. The rarity and eternal elegance of vintage watches make a stark contrast to the masses; understatement and classic design give them a much subtler hint of taste in the face of a thousand shameless identical declarations of wealth. An investment-grade vintage watch is an asset whose cultural and monetary values are virtually immune to fashion, at least over the long run.

Excursus: The Lifesaving Rise of Mechanical Wristwatches

For decades, wristwatches have been omnipresent in our lives, and we treat them as totally normal. Yet, history tells an interesting story about the emergence of the mechanical wristwatch in the first place, long before being threatened by the quartz movement. Mechanical watches first gained importance on wrists during a much darker period of history: in the 1910s, more precisely during World War I. Having to fumble around in one's pocket for old-fashioned pocket watches with dials that were difficult to read while being in the middle of combat on land or in the air was inconvenient at best, lethal at worst for soldiers and officers. Being able to read the time directly from one's wrist was a feature that soon became very much in demand and marked the beginning of the end of the pocket watch era. Only two decades later, during World War II, the more luxurious versions of mechanical watches proved to have another, potentially life-saving, feature: British Royal Air Force pilots used to wear luxury watches to protect themselves when things turned against them by keeping them as the last option to bribe themselves out of war captivity.

What Really Makes an Investment?

Let us briefly look at the concept of an investment. We all know the term and use it frequently in our daily lives. Some tend to say to friends even their new 60-inch TV is an *investment*. But what really makes an investment and differentiates it from pure consumption? And how do watches fit in the framework of this concept? First, the textbook definition:

"An investment is an asset or item acquired with the goal of generating income or appreciation. In an economic sense, an investment is the purchase of goods that are not consumed today but are used in the future to create wealth. In finance, an investment is a monetary asset purchased with the idea that the asset will provide income in the future or will later be sold at a higher price for a profit."

(Investopedia, 2018).

So when speaking about an investment we need to look at wealth creation (rather than consumption) through *income* or *capital appreciation*. Traditional assets such as real estate, stocks, or bonds, for example, can provide on the one hand income or yield in the form of dividends, rental income, or interest and, on the other hand, might also appreciate in value. These conventional assets thereby fulfill both parts of the definition and are clearly investments. Hence, the core of your financial planning should clearly be based on a diversified portfolio of real estate, stocks, bonds and maybe some precious metals or digital assets. So far, so good. Watches, however, similar to precious metals like gold or other real assets such as artworks, can only fulfill the second part of the definition as they do not offer a continuous income stream.

And here we have already established one of the most commonly cited downsides of investing in watches: the lack of steady income or yield. This attribute makes investing available funds in this new asset class less attractive for certain groups of investors. Imagine, for example, a retired couple who seeks to live from a steady income stream as large as possible and does not want to wait for long-term capital gains. Should this couple diversify part of their traditional yield and dividend-oriented core portfolio of stocks and bonds and also invest in watches? It depends, but I would argue only if it also seeks portfolio diversification and tail-risk protection benefits.

Some experts in the industry argue that this strict and rather dry definition does not tell the whole story of an investment. In addition to the textbook wording, we also need to add one very crucial layer when analyzing watches as an investment. While there is no monetary income stream such as a cash dividend, buyers of vintage watches enjoy a form of *non-pecuniary dividends*, i.e. the intellectual and emotional stimulation from possessing, and possibly wearing, the investment piece. In short, owning the watch creates pleasure.

"Whether collecting for passion, profit or some combination of the two, fine art and other collectibles constitute an asset class unlike any other."
(Morgan Stanley, 2019)

This is why watches fall into the category of so-called passion investments. To be clear, we don't use this term in a diminishing or inferiority-implying way compared to non-passion investments (although I understand the connotation sometimes suggests this).

While falling in love with a particular investment (such as a specific stock) is usually not a good thing, falling in love with an asset class and the process of investing in this asset class itself is an undeniable recipe for success. Listen to any great investor talking about their profession and life as an investor—no matter whether it's Donald Bren, Joel Greenblatt or Howard Marks. You can easily hear how passionate they are about their specific asset class or investing niche, no matter whether it's real estate (Bren), value stocks (Greenblatt) or distressed fixed-income assets (Marks). In reality,

24

the value appreciation potential alone should be appealing enough for investors to justify investing in watches, leaving alone the protective diversification layer that one adds to his portfolio with this real asset. The passion factor should be seen as an additional advantage that might convince potential watch investors on the brink who need a final push to convince them to start their very first watch portfolio.

"Auction houses traditionally say they're selling you an object that you buy with your heart, because you love it. It's a bit of a blinkered view. I don't think people should be afraid of talking about investment values. We do it about our houses, why not watches? Investment is a bit of a dirty word, but for vintage watches in this country it's the biggest growth area."
– James Marks, (Barber, 2020)

Institutions ranging from Ultra-high-net-worth individual private banks such as Coutts to the private wealth departments of international banks such as Morgan Stanley classify watches as one of the most important passion investment assets alongside classic cars, antiques, artworks, and rare whiskey and wine. We heard that one of the core aspects of passion investments is that they provide their investors with pleasure and offer a sort of replacement yield from that pleasure. As real assets, on top, they typically offer inflation protection and tail-risk protection in case of an economic crisis or a *black swan event* that poses an unexpected shock for traditional asset markets (think subprime crisis or Covid-19). Moreover, it shall be noted that there is always a positive value larger than zero in any passion asset.

If a stock is, for example, subject to severe fraud and goes to zero (think Enron) or a bond issuer declares bankruptcy and liquidation follows, there is not much that can be done with the acquired security. However, even in the unlikely case that a particular watch you identified as investment-grade becomes suddenly totally out of demand and neglected by the whole watch investment world, there is still an appealing fallback option: you can still

25

pass the passion asset on to your next generation and preserve the family legacy. Undeniably better than passing over a worthless piece of paper implying stock ownership of a company that ceased to exist.

All in all, investing in watches and other passion assets is a special kind of intellectual and cultural stimulation that mankind always needed and always will continue to seek. Like art or classic cars, watches are the essence of culture, and passion-driven investing is deeply rooted in our human nature. And while the term passion might suggest that purchases are not conducted objectively and determined purely by emotion, this could not be further from the truth. Surely, watch investors fall for the same behavioral biases as investors in other asset classes. However, while many investors in assets such as stocks are not fully aware of it, being 100 percent aware of your passion for the underlying asset class does help to control your behavioral biases and to counteract them.

A watch investor knows that he tends to fall in love too easily with his assets, which enables him to take steps to avoid mistakes proactively.

Investor or Collector?

When speaking about watches, you very quickly arrive at one question: are you an investor or collector? But what exactly differentiates these two, sometimes interchangeably used, terms?

"Collecting and investment go hand in hand. At the moment I think people still collect watches because they are attracted to the aesthetics of them, and the investment side isn't really spoken about."
— James Marks, (Foulkes, 2018)

The majority of watch enthusiasts who own more than two or three classic watches would describe themselves primarily as a collector. However, some collectors might think they share features of an investor. If true, this would make them an *investor-collector,* a term that consultancy Capgemini introduced first in their World Wealth Report a few years back—an assumption that might well be true but very often is not. When looking at the buying and selling patterns of many of my friends who I know see themselves as investor-collectors, only a handful of them actually fall into that category. Why is that?

No matter whether we are talking baseball cards or vintage watches, a collector follows one of the most ancient human instincts. He is searching either systematically or unsystematically for material to trade, originally in order to survive. The completeness of the collection is crucial for the systematic collector but less important for the unsystematic collector (who collects whatever he likes with a larger degree of randomness). Some die-hard collectors even diametrically oppose the concept that their collection might increase in value. Such behavior might well bring a lot of non-pecuniary dividends, but the financial gains are typically insufficient for the needs of a financially oriented investor who seeks sound, risk-adjusted returns. Moreover, a purist collection might come at the expense of

27

portfolio liquidity in moments when it is most crucially needed (e.g. to purchase the grail watch).

Still, collectors play a highly important role in the watch market and are one of the most crucial driving forces behind supply and demand. Even if not all collectors openly think about watches in a financial way, especially high-value collectors who buy watches for several tens and hundreds of thousands of dollars, are certainly thinking very carefully about what their acquired watches might be worth a few years down the road—consciously or unconsciously. It may not be their primary motivation, but it is certainly a key factor behind their actions. And let's be frank—even when a collector acquires a piece that he truly loves, only very rarely will he keep the piece for eternity without ever considering selling.

"I won't call them collectors, because they're not."
– James Mark's [on the new generation of watch buyers]
(Barber, 2020)

In fact, the most sophisticated collectors know at any given point in time during their ownership of a watch whether it was a good investment. In practice, many collectors do regularly keep track of their watch portfolio using various tools and closely track dealer prices and recent auction results to re-evaluate their portfolio constantly in rough terms. And anecdotal evidence showed me: the *investment factor* is even more crucial than you might think at first. Many collectors might even lose interest or fall out of love with some pieces of their collection in the (hypothetical) case that this additional justification layer would suddenly disappear.

"I think people who say they're collectors and not investors are somewhat naïve" [...] *"They're putting money into something they've worked incredibly hard to earn, and if said watch or car was suddenly worth zero, they certainly wouldn't be happy. In the same vein, I think they're the same people who, when they sell for a profit, don't tell their friends how*

28

disappointed they are to let it go, but rather how much money they made from it!"

– James Marks (Easthope, 2019)

What sounds crazy at first is a pervasive theme I observed among several high-profile collectors. The psychology behind this is simple, yet intriguing: it is the ego-charming magic mirror of confirmation that tells the collector he has put together a masterpiece collection of tremendous worth; a self-esteem boost, which is often key to the mindset of a collector, making him—often unconsciously and without his explicit knowledge—also an investor.

Investor or Speculator?

Another term that often arises quickly when talking about investments in passion assets is *speculation*. The textbook definition of this everyday term that carries, without doubt, a negative connotation is:

"Speculation is the act of trading in an asset [...] that has a significant risk of losing most or all of the initial outlay with the expectation of a substantial gain [...]."

(Investopedia, 2020)

Watch investing is sometimes wrongly compared to speculation. This could not be further from the truth. Speculation usually comprises a short holding period (several days or weeks, maybe sometimes a few months) and often involves leverage. Both of these parameters are in stark contrast to watch investing, which is a no-leverage (you hardly ever should take on a loan to buy an investment watch), long-term game. Done the right way, investing in watches is not a high-risk, high-return matter. However, there is one exception that is very often confused with investing: *flipping* watches.

This speculative activity relates primarily to contemporary models that are, albeit still in production, very hard to get (at retail price) and boast a long waiting list, oftentimes up to a decade or more. This sort of short-term trading is essentially retail arbitrage. It can be highly profitable in theory; however, it has several practical constraints (which I will clarify in a few minutes). Depending on the way flipping it is conducted, it would fall either into the category of speculation or true arbitrage, i.e. virtually riskless profit from taking advantage of price dislocations. The bottom line is that there are only very few similarities to speculation-driven asset classes and—leaving the practice of watch flipping aside—the unique characteristics of (vintage) watches make a strong case for the investment merits of this young asset class.

Contemporary or Vintage?

I cannot count the number of times I have found myself at a dinner party or after-work event where I was shown a brand-new modern-day watch (bought at retail price) and asked what I thought of it as an investment. Sure, most contemporary watches from the likes of Breitling, Panerai, or IWC are amazingly engineered objects of desire. They offer cutting-edge mechanical technology and rarely ever will let their owner down. However, when it comes to the softer aspects like history, romance, or collectability, the majority of contemporary pieces very quickly fall short—with immediate effects on their status as a potential investment. As mentioned before, more than 95 percent of all watches are not investable. The majority of them are stunning luxury goods to own, consume, and enjoy but neither retain value nor make good investments. Some might argue this does not hold true for brands like Rolex or Patek Philippe, and limited editions and great brand storytelling solve parts of the problem. While partially true, in the long-term nothing can replace the rarity and history of vintage timepieces. Vintage watches have and will always have a decades-long jumpstart ahead of their contemporary rivals.

Excursus: Parallels between a Ferrari GTO and a COMEX Submariner
If you think about the question of whether to invest in contemporary or vintage watches, it pretty much boils down to common sense. A brand-new Ferrari 488 is amazing yet much less desirable than a 1960 Ferrari GTO of which only a handful of cars were made, and they hold a remarkable place in the history of car marking. You can draw direct comparisons to the watch world where the rare Rolex Submariner COMEX Ref. 5514 will always be more precious than the brand-new, modern-day factory model. It should be common sense for the purist investor to go primarily after vintage models as investments and only occasionally add in a contemporary piece—either with amazing growth prospects or to actually wear on a day-to-day basis.

Let's jump to Miami for a second, where my friend Pablo lives. He is all over watches and is a collector of both contemporary and vintage watches. Pablo is a proponent of vintage pieces in terms of their investment merits. However, he absolutely loves to buy modern limited editions and reissues because they give him the possibility to wear a contemporary interpretation of an iconic piece (that sometimes also sits in his safe deposit box). Thus he can trust in modern shock and water-resistance features and still enjoy a revamped, yet classic design. His everyday watch is currently an Audemars Piguet Royal Oak Ref. 15202, but he also owns a A-Series Ref. 5402 Jumbo with a lovely tropical dial. Pablo is a prime example that elitist rules no longer hold true in the watch world and that the lines between contemporary and vintage watches are ever more blurring. While one can embrace both worlds, the purist investor will be better off focusing on vintage pieces. Contemporary pieces can be a way to enrich your portfolio and wear the watch design you desire—just the way Pablo does it. However, you must be aware that in an overwhelming number of cases the hard reality is that, aside from a relatively small handful of models, brand-new contemporary watches do not provide a promising fundament for the vast majority of a portfolio—at least compared to their vintage counterparts.

Excursus: Why You Cannot Make Money Flipping Watches

Enter Rolex in the year 2021. Today, many Rolex men's professional steel sports models have the fame (or infamy) of virtually doubling in value on the pre-owned market seconds after they have left the store. In fact, some models have become so popular and in-demand that stainless steel models have become more valuable than their equivalent precious metal counterparts. At least, in theory, there is a way to make money from this bubble-like phenomenon we see in modern-day Rolex watches. Let's call it "queue-cutting"—and it's all about access: avoiding the famous waitlists (or moving onto preferred client lists) and using your connections to get highly sought-after dealer allocations money cannot (easily) buy. In theory this is a profitable business model that also works equally well with Patek Philippe or Audemars Piguet. It would allow you to acquire a hot Audemars Piguet Royal Oak Jumbo (Ref. 15202ST) or Rolex GMT-Master II Pepsi (Ref. 126710BLRO) at retail price and shortly thereafter sell it at a nice arbitrage-like profit. For both of these models, prices in the pre-owned market lie significantly above retail prices due to the limited availability of these high-demand, relatively low-production watches. If somebody does not want to spend a lengthy period of time on a waitlist (or buy their way into preferred client status) but wear that same watch next weekend, he will pay an "availability premium" in the secondary market.

Especially over the past couple of years, incredible premia are being paid, often up to 100 percent or more. The problem with this flipping strategy is that in order to get these allocations not once but constantly you need to be a good customer, ideally a VIP customer. This equals to having a lot of money spent at your AD. Sure, you could get lucky and get a Rolex Starbucks (Ref. 126610LV) allocation after some years of waiting, even without spending thousands of dollars before at the AD. But to constantly get allocations to hot models, usually the purchase of no-so-hot models and a long history and relationship with the dealer are required. Moreover, the AD will typically want to make sure that he can trust you and that you are not a watch flipper. So while it is, in theory, a worthwhile gamble, even one quick-flip trade can ruin your slowly (and expensively) built relationship with your AD. This obviously doesn't mean that you can never ever sell any of your hot watches, but you hopefully get the point that it is much more difficult to constantly make money from flipping brand new watches than the theory might suggest.

Who Should Invest in Watches?

"An expert is an ordinary man away from home giving advice."

— Oscar Wilde

So after reading this first couple of pages, one question should inevitably arise at the top of your head: if the arguments for investing in watches are so appealing, should everybody allocate a proportion of his wealth or savings to watches? The answer is a clear No. And here is why: investing in watches is a very slow and thorough process. While some of the advantages of wealth allocation to watches (i.e. portfolio diversification or non-pecuniary dividends) will provide incredible benefits for folks with at least a basic interest in the subject and asset class, this might not be the case if you are a purist die-hard financial investor with zero interest in watches. If you picked up this book because you are solely interested in cross-asset portfolio diversification and lack any enthusiasm for watches, this guide is probably already boring you to death at this stage. Investing in watches in this case might not be something you should seriously consider. And this is totally fine. There are plenty of other alternative asset classes that provide similar, and at times even better, diversification and inflation-protection benefits. Maybe art, classic cars or rare whiskey—if that is more your thing. Or you may decide to completely stay away from passion investments and stick with traditional means of investing and wealth planning via real estate, stocks, etc.

"While I wouldn't necessarily advocate putting one's entire life savings into any one commodity, adding some quality watches into your investment portfolio is anything but crazy."

— James Lamdin, CEO of Analog Shift (Andhora, 2018)

In the watch world, the lack of uniformity, the existence of transaction costs and the range of other pitfalls are often too complex and time-consuming for an investor who is not willing to make a deep dive into the history, complications, and investment dynamics of a certain reference. It's simply not just about the numbers. Investments in this extraordinary asset class require a higher level of vigilance and involvement from the investor, at least compared with certain other asset classes. To justify this sort of high engagement without being a watch enthusiast is tough, especially since we are not talking about the majority of your portfolio (which should sit in stocks, bonds and real estate) but only about a relatively small allocation of your net worth (as mentioned, five percent is a decent starting point). Hence, it should become clear that maintaining a watch investment portfolio must provide its owner with pleasure and create additional emotional dividends to justify the undertaking. The fact that an investor in this asset class has to be knowledgeable about a pyramidal market, the evaluation of non-uniform assets, the specifics of the due diligence process and the interactions among its limited, often powerful market makers and key players means therefore that you should only invest in watches if you receive at least some degree of pleasure from being so deeply engaged.

Will it ultimately pay off? Unfortunately, I also do not own a crystal ball. However, I can say with a large degree of confidence that for an *involved* investor—who is willing to go the extra mile and develop a real interest in and knowledge of watches—an intelligently put together portfolio of (vintage) watches will not only have an extremely high chance of outperforming ultra-low interest rates in savings accounts by miles but will also act as a great portfolio diversifier, especially in times of crisis as high-quality inflation-proof vintage timepieces will always be somewhat ringfenced from economic downturns.

"I think there's a lot of money sitting on the sidelines that will start to look at watches [...]. It is inevitable that institutional and hedge fund money will explore investing in collections of historical importance or rarity."

– James Marks (Foulkes, 2018)

To get another opinion on this, enter Canada-born Kevin O'Leary. The venture capitalist, CNBC expert and *Shark Tank* TV host has invested in virtually all asset classes out there, but when publicly discussing his investments, he considers his watch portfolio to be the best-performing among all of them. *"This asset class outperformed everything in the last five years"*, growing at least 400 percent, O'Leary told his audience at the ANC's Leadership Forum in 2018. To be successful, you don't have to be as enthusiastic as watch-nerd O'Leary, but if you like watches and are willing to do the work, you should also invest in them.

"Conventional wisdom on collecting vintage watches 15 or 20 years ago was to buy with your heart, not your head—meaning if you buy what you love it can never be a bad investment. It's a wonderful sentiment, and one I subscribe to, at least in part. But the difference today, of course, is that values in vintage have come up tremendously, and are continuing to do so year over year. In my view, if you're spending serious money, be it $2,000, $20,000 or $200,000 on a watch, you'd better involve your head in the equation!"

– James Lamdin (Andhora, 2018)

Part I – Chapter Summary:

- While the majority of your wealth allocation should sit in more traditional financial assets such as real estate, stocks, bonds (and maybe crypto), timepieces are *passion assets* that can diversify a portfolio
- Done rightly, watches can be alternative investments with great risk-rewards dynamics, not just speculation objects
- While in theory it is possible to make arbitrage-like profits from flipping hot contemporary watches, there are several practical constraints
- Investing in watches is not for everyone. If the subject bores you, you might rather gift this book away than trying to invest successfully in this asset class
- Most collectors think like investors—at least from time to time

Part II: Watch Investing Fundamentals

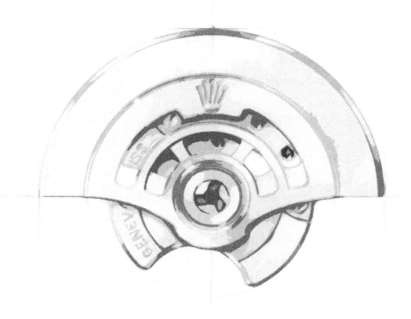

The Rules of the Game

S imilar to more traditional investments such as stocks or real estate, investment-grade timepieces boast an array of unique investment highlights.

These are distinct features tied to every specific asset class. Also watches have several such characteristics that define them as their own distinct alternative asset class. We will now look at the most important asset class characteristics to see what they can do to enrich your personal portfolio.

The 8 benefits of watches as an alternative asset class are as follows:

- Safe-haven status
- Fungibility
- Privacy
- Market inefficiency
- Decorrelation & diversification
- Capital appreciation
- Tax efficiency
- Non-pecuniary dividends

Safe-Haven Status

Watches are real assets—tangible objects that can serve as a *safe-haven* in periods of stress in other markets. A safe-haven asset provides investors with protection against market turbulence and limits exposure in recessionary or bear market phases. Safe-havens usually profit or retain their value in times of increased volatility of other asset markets, particularly during stock market downturns and economic crises. Put bluntly, when a bubble bursts and everything else falls, safe-haven assets such as investment-grade watches stay rather uncorrelated to the general market environment as investors seek them as a tangible store of value. Similarly to physical or digital gold, watches can serve as a sort of insurance policy against adverse economic events or an acute threat of (hyper-) inflation. Over the years, brands such as Patek Philippe in particular have created an atmosphere of government bond-like investability around its timepieces. Consider the geopolitical escalation of the trade war between the USA and China during late 2018 that resulted in a sharp drop in global stock markets around Christmas Eve. While most asset classes were heavily correlated and dropped sharply, prices for investment-grade watches moved the opposite way. Their price movements were decorrelated to the stock and bond markets. A similar tendency could be observed in early 2020 when the world became increasingly aware that Covid-19 would spread rapidly around the globe and asset markets tanked in unison. In such difficult times, investors and wealthy individuals alike take refuge in safe-havens to avoid large amplitudes of volatility in other markets or hold them as means of inflation protection. But a partial allocation of your net worth to investment-grade, high-quality vintage watches has not only benefits if you have ten digits on your bank account statement. Even small cross-asset portfolios can benefit significantly from a partial allocation to investment-grade timepieces.

"Faced with economic uncertainty and volatile stock markets, people tend to invest in tangible assets such as precious metals, jewelry and timepieces to diversify their portfolios. Vintage watches can be a safe investment and those that are particularly rare can enhance a collector's investment portfolio providing diversification and store of value."

(Credit Suisse, 2020)

However, while certain kinds of watches are nearly as tangible and provide the same safety function as gold, the characteristics of these two asset classes are quite different. Most importantly, gold has a fixed quoted price that is publicly available to all market participants on a second-by-second basis. It acts as a medium of exchange because of its singularity and comparability. One pure 10-ounce gold bar is absolutely identical to another (leaving geological and chemical details aside). This is not the case for one Patek Philippe watch and another, even if reference, age, and origin are the same on paper. In fact, the differences between each watch can vary so widely that it is not unheard of for a watch with the same reference but different condition or provenance to demand only a tenth of the price of its counterpart. The beauty of watches as an asset class is that they are increasingly likely to preserve value during times of stress and outperform in periods of market volatility.

While statistical and academic work on the subject is rare, the few available studies prove that watches made tremendous investments in the past because, as an asset, they are surprisingly resilient and non-volatile. A recent 10-year asset price volatility study by luxury specialist broker Knight Frank placed watches second in terms of non-volatility, only losing to collectible furniture. So, while watches might not be the most rapidly appreciating of all alternative assets, they are surely among the least volatile ones. This stunningly low volatility compares not only very favorably to the stock market but even to other safe-haven assets such as gold.

Fungibility

In economics, *fungibility* means that equal units of a certain good are interchangeable. While other safe-haven assets such as physical gold are more fungible (i.e. they can be exchanged quicker for their dollar equivalent), the small size and low weight of a watch make it advantageous compared to many alternatives such as rare whiskey, artworks or classic cars. Watches are certainly not the most moveable goods but also not the worst. In case of an emergency situation, you definitely can cross a border easier with a rare Patek Philippe perpetual calendar on your wrist than with a Mark Rothko painting under your arm. Among their attractions is also the fact that—thanks to the increasingly digital market—investment-grade watches, especially the most liquid mid-priced pieces, are sold very quickly, often within only a few days or even hours. This is seldom the case for artworks for example.

Privacy

Watches can be bought in near-perfect *privacy* and anonymity. Demand for such privacy will increase as we live in times when the privacy of wealth comes under increased scrutiny. Here, precious watches can step in and help at least somewhat to counteract that development. The reasons why someone would seek more privacy in investments are manifold. Compliant with the local tax laws and regulations in your country of residence watches can offer a way to store a portion of your wealth in a much more private and anonymous way than many other assets.

Market Inefficiency

When discussing asset markets, efficiency describes the extent to which publicly available information is already incorporated into the price of assets trading in that market. For investors, this degree of efficiency is an important measure because it also gives a good indication as to whether it is possible to beat any given market. The concept was initially researched by Nobel prize awarded economist Eugene Fama in the 1970s in the context of the stock market. Fama established the so-called Efficient Market Hypothesis for the stock market. According to Fama, stocks should trade at their fair value, making it theoretically impossible for investors to buy stocks below or sell stocks above their value. In other words, if all available information about an asset is properly reflected in its price, it is impossible to beat the market. Of course, there are many opponents of Fama's theory, and rightly so. Most certainly, there are phases and niches in the stock market where information is more or less efficient. Just think about small-cap stocks or complex sectors such as biotechnology.

But what about efficiency in the watch market? Fortunately, this field is much more clear-cut: without exaggerating, compared to most other asset markets, the investment-grade watch market is even nowadays nothing less than an oasis of *inefficiency*. This enormous inefficiency mainly arises from four factors: lack of institutionalization, behavioral constraints, liquidity constraints, and—to a lesser extent—movability. Let us tackle them one by one. First, a major efficiency constraint in the watch market is the *lack of institutionalization*. Contrary to the stock market, for example, there are still virtually no (except a few) professional full-time investors in watches and these do lack significant scale. This is a crucial advantage if you want to achieve a certain information advantage, also called *edge*, in any market. Secondly, the presence of collectors who don't always act rationally and are not driven by the same motives—neither among themselves nor in comparison to purely return-driven investors—is a so-called *behavioral constraint*. Furthermore, the lack of one specific market to buy and sell, such as the New York Stock Exchange, makes it increasingly difficult to efficiently match buyers and sellers and drives down overall *liquidity*. Last but not least is the more problematic *movability* of watches as hard assets compared to digital paper trades, such as those done with stocks for example. The inevitable consequence is the emergence of regional trading hubs that are much less efficient. Put all this together and you get an unusually high degree of inefficiency.

Excursus: A Tale on Extreme Inefficiency

In Summer 2004, one day I was walking around the flea market in St. Tropez, France, on Place des Lices. It was a Saturday morning, and I was checking out the usually amazing vintage furniture offerings. I love to look there for antiques (yet hardly ever bought anything), but I also always had an eye for the vintage watch offerings. I do love to examine the hard-beaten WWII-era watches that you can find here from time to time. But this very morning, it has been different. I looked at one stand that I had never discovered before (at least I could not recall it) and spotted a watch from some meters away, in classical Rolex dive watch trim. The watch was lacking a bracelet and had clear signs of wear and tear, especially on the heavily scratched glass, but at first glance, the watch looked still in decent shape. I stepped closer to find that the watch was a Tudor. I asked if I could see it and whether it was working. It was hard to tell the reference on the spot, but given the resemblance to a Rolex Ref. 5512, I was reasonably sure that in effect, I had a Tudor Submariner Ref. 7928 from the mid-1960s in my hand! Somewhat absent and with the expectancy of a phantasy price I asked in French "How much would you like for the watch?" The seller, about a 60-year old man, wearing a linen shirt and red worn-out Grimaud Yacht Club hat, got back to me in Provençal accent: "It's, 200 Euro". There was no way that the seller would not recognize a Tudor, so I had to ask him to repeat the price. The dial under the scratched glass seemed actually in pretty good shape, and although I was sure that it might be some sort of Franken watch, I had a feeling that the impossible might be possible. "Do such good replicas of vintage Tudors exist?" I was asking myself with various thoughts jumbling through my head. Suddenly, I concluded that the dial was just too perfectly aged to be a replica. "Okay. I will take it then", I told the man in French after he repeated the price, and the watch was starting to run. Without wanting to draw too much attention, I pretended to be less excited, paid the 200 Euro

44

in cash, thanked the happy seller and walked away. Less than 50 meters away from the market, I immediately turned right into the next little side street, ordered a noisette at a small bistro, and started to examine the watch in detail on the patio. I didn't have any tools with me and needed to wait to return home two weeks later before I was able to open the watch. Back home, I checked the movement and disassembled the watch completely. I could not believe that I had bought a real Tudor Snowflake Ref. 7928, distinguished by its square crown guards, for 200 bucks! As mentioned, the watch was somewhat distressed and usually and at a normal price wouldn't be suitable as an investment for me, due to its condition, but for this bargain price even the slightly distressed exterior condition, need for a replacement bracelet, a full service, and a new glass were no problem at all. I ended up fitting the watch with a NATO strap and gifted it to one of my best friends at his wedding, who I knew was in love with the story and charm of this marvelous, worn-down beater.

Inefficiency peaks that offer such extreme buying opportunities have always been rare, but the rise of the internet has made them become even rarer. Yet, the point that I am trying to make is that the watch market is still incredibly inefficient when comparing it to other asset classes! When was the last time someone offered you an ounce of gold for significantly less than its fair value? In the watch market such things happen all the time. While you should not necessarily expect to get lucky at your local flea market (it is still worth the occasional try, although my view will forever remain biased), I guarantee you that buying at a discount to true value is still possible in this asset class. Sure, with the ascent of the digital economy, it has become increasingly more difficult as the information everybody is working on has gotten just so much better. But still, be it at large scale auctions in Geneva or in the window of a small dealer in Rome, we are still far away from the efficiency of other asset markets.

Decorrelation & Diversification

Technically speaking, *correlation* in investing is a measure of how much two or more assets move in relation to each other. Whenever assets increase or decline in value at the same point in time, they are correlated. In turn, whenever one asset declines (or stays stable) while the other increases, two assets are negatively correlated. Academic research on passion investments in relation to the global stock market has been a mixed bag. Some behavioral finance researchers argue that a stock market's boom or bull market positively influences passion assets since investors are allocating part of their profits from stocks to other assets, including watches. It makes intuitive sense that a rational investor might want to take some money off the table and move it to a different assets class after an extended bull market phase in the stock market. There would obviously remain a certain lag effect, but the watch market should stay positively correlated to the equity market if this hypothesis holds true. However, history shows us that this is only true for short-term market swings. On the contrary, in the long run the watch market is much less correlated to the equity market than most other asset classes.

In this regard, we can take a look at watch auctions during the time of the global financial crisis of 2008/09. Interestingly, watch auctions proved surprisingly stable while financial markets and the global economy were struggling with the downturn caused by the collapse of the subprime real estate bubble and its aftermath. Total auction volumes were down; however, this was largely due to the hesitance of sellers to consign certain high-value lots directly after the Lehman Brothers turmoil in autumn 2008, not necessarily due to a lack of demand. For Christie's and Sotheby's, the sell-through rates, i.e. the percentage of lots sold indicated by the number of lots or by their value, proved exceptionally strong during and after the crisis—they exceeded 90 percent for Christie's and 80 percent for Sotheby's. Actual sale prices outperformed auction house expectations often by two to three times during that time. As a direct consequence, in a 2010 feature of the *New York Times*, Phillips star auctioneer Aurel Bacs called 2009 a *"spectacular year"*. Astonishingly enough, the first auctions in

46

2009 showed a market that was hungry for vintage watches despite having the financial world collapse around it. Rare vintage watches and exceptional modern pieces did equally well.

"Besides impassioned collectors, weary investors appeared to be taking refuge in watches from volatile equity markets and fears of inflation."

– Trent Crowley, CEO of online auctioneer Astorlive
(Lankarani, 2010)

Recent reports suggest that history repeats itself also during the Covid-19 crisis, with online auctions being the big lockdown winner this time. At the time of this writing in spring 2020, several dealers were already putting together portfolios of investment-grade Rolex and Patek Philippe for some of their clients who are seeking to park money, both as a tail-risk equity market hedge and as protection against uncontrollable central bank helicopter money that was released in order to fight a looming economic recession. Recently run online auctions by Sotheby's, usually reserved for lower value watches, experienced an unprecedented rise in demand. In April 2020, Sotheby's launched a new weekly format that immediately proved successful. In the two consecutive weeks when the global pandemic reached new heights back then, the auction house twice broke a new record for its most expensive watch sold online.

"Originally online [auctions were] for lower price points for our business," *[...]. "But in the last month"—as the pandemic spread globally—"we've really exponentially moved up the curve."*

– Josh Pullan, Managing Director of Sotheby's Watches
(Wolf, 2020)

While decorrelation can be a great thing to have in general, it only unfolds its full power in a broader portfolio context. In modern portfolio theory, one can minimize the overall risk of a portfolio of investments by adding assets that move in different directions. This means that by adding less-correlated assets such as watches to your portfolio, you carry less risk and should do relatively better in any given market environment, keeping your wealth more diversified.

"From my earlier failures, I knew that no matter how confident I was in making any one bet I could still be wrong—and that proper diversification was the key to reducing risks without reducing returns. If I could build [a portfolio filled with high-quality return streams that were] properly diversified (they zigged and zagged in ways that balanced each other out), I could offer clients an overall portfolio return much more consistent and reliable than what they could get elsewhere."

– Ray Dalio, Founder of Bridgewater Associates
(Simon & Schuster, 2017)

Ray Dalio, the founder of Bridgewater Associates, one of the most successful hedge funds, refers to this theory of diversification and uncorrelated return streams as the holy grail of investing. Although Dalio didn't invent this concept and it was not meant to be applied to watches, referring to uncorrelated asset return streams, is, in fact, absolutely applicable to investment-grade watches as well. In essence, you are removing peaks and troughs and flattening out your portfolio return curve. Your portfolio might not always outperform in a bull market rally, but you certainly will sleep better whenever the stock markets turn sour again.

Adding a significantly less or uncorrelated asset such as watches to your average 60/40 stock/bond portfolio provides undeniable diversification benefits by reducing correlation. Such diversification across assets is often referred to as the only free lunch in investing. And smart diversification is a cornerstone to build a sustainable, long-term portfolio where each asset—stock, bonds, real estate, gold, crypto and watches—performs in a different manner and the outperformance of one asset class at any given point cushions any potential losses of another class throughout the whole economic cycle.

Capital Appreciation

Due to the lack of centralized, uniform information, it is difficult to assess the investment returns of watches as a whole asset class over time like we can do for the stock or bond market. However, one can look at studies by wealth specialists such as renowned (private) banks Credit Suisse and Coutts or luxury broker Knight Frank, at aggregated secondary data from brokerage platforms such as Chrono24 as well as at anecdotal reference from auctions. The data problem arises mainly from the decentralized nature of watch transactions. Watches are sold in public, semi-public and private transactions. While it is possible to assess single watch values by doing individual research and get a reasonable understanding of the price developments of certain timepieces, it is more difficult to accurately track the return profile of the asset class as a whole. Luxury specialist Knight Frank provides in his Wealth Report a yearly attempt to capture the returns from auctions and put them a single number. Their latest 2020 report shows that watches as a whole asset class have appreciated on average 89 percent over the last ten years—an annualized return of roughly 6.5 percent. And already in their first report back in 2013 Knight Frank reported a 76 percent gain since 2003. Coutts, the private bank of choice for ultra-high-net-worth individuals, underlines these numbers in their yearly Passion Index according to which watches look back to an annual return of more than 6 percent since the launch of the Coutts index in 2005. In Fall 2020, Swiss bank Credit Suisse showed in its inaugural study in collaboration with Deloitte very similar returns for the asset class of (wrist) watches, in fact 5.5 percent annualized since 1983, and compared these returns to various plain-vanilla and alternative asset classes. When looking at the data (below), it becomes clear: from a risk-reward perspective (i.e. comparing returns with volatility) wrist watches do play in the Champions League, clearly outpacing the risk profiles of many other (more) popular asset classes.

Of course, statistics like these always have to be read with a pinch of salt. Aside from the financial crisis in 2008/09 and the European sovereign debt crisis, in the last two decades we sure do look back to a period of constant economic upturn accompanied by interest rates at historic lows. One might argue that rising prices in virtually all other asset classes—the *everything bubble* as some call it—also had its effect on the watch market.

Table 1: Historical returns and volatilities

	Annualized returns	Annualized volatility (std. dev.)	Returns to volatility ratio
Wine index (Liv-ex100, 2001–20)	5.7%	12.9%	43.9%
HAGI (R) Top Index (2010–20)	12.0%	10.1%	119.1%
Sotheby's Mei Moses All Art Index (1950–2019)	8.4%	16.9%	49.7%
Contemporary art	9.4%	35.3%	26.5%
Impressionist and modern art	8.9%	33.8%	26.2%
Old master and 19th century art	7.4%	19.1%	38.8%
British paintings	9.1%	50.1%	18.2%
American art	6.7%	37.0%	18.2%
Latin American art	12.2%	39.1%	31.2%
Traditional Chinese works of art	6.5%	22.0%	29.6%
Art Market Research Jewelry and Watches Index (jewelry indices: 1985–2020, wristwatches: 1983–2020, pocket watches: 1976–2020)			
Jewelry: Post-war up to 1975	4.8%	2.4%	196.7%
Jewelry: Art deco and pearls	5.0%	2.4%	211.8%
Watches: Wrist	5.5%	3.4%	160.0%
Watches: Pocket	1.5%	2.9%	51.1%
Art Market Research Luxury Handbag Index (2010–20)			
Luxury handbags: Chanel	6.0%	3.5%	170.0%
Luxury handbags: Hermès Birkin	5.7%	6.9%	82.1%
Selected traditionnal asset classes			
Global equities (MSCI AC World, 1976–2020)	7.7%	15.1%	51%
Global bonds (1990–2020)	5.6%	5.3%	107%
US Govt. long-term bonds (1976–2020)	8.8%	10.8%	82%
US corporate bonds (1976–2020)	7.9%	6.8%	116%
Developed market real estate (1994–2020)	6.3%	19.2%	33%
Commodities (1976–2020)	4.8%	14.9%	32%
Gold (1976–2020)	6.1%	18.6%	33%
Hedge funds (1993–2020)	7.0%	6.8%	104%

(Credit Suisse, 2020)

Today, watches are not more bubbly than other asset classes, but we should appreciate that the flight out of other asset classes (and gains taken from the table) has certainly had an additional return-enhancing effect over the last decade. Fueled by a range of factors such rising rarity of the most precious timepieces, record-level quantitative easing and money printing by central banks, and desperate investors that seek new alternative avenues for their capital, global valuations of vintage and contemporary watches have known only one direction for years, with nearly every major watch auction accompanied by headlines of sellers achieving new record price profits. It won't go on forever like this. At least not at this speed. But while past performance is never a guarantee of future returns, the attractiveness of the asset class has been clearly on the rise and watches have not appreciated in a stable fashion by 5-6 percent per year over the last decades without reason. In fact, for a skilled watch investor these mid-single digit annualized returns are even on the conservative side as they look at the overall market as a whole and do not include any brand focus, selective due diligence or financially-savvy portfolio construction.

So what returns are possible in the watch world? It all depends on your skill (and some luck), but only one or two very good investments can catapult your returns clearly into very different spheres. We all heard of the record-breaking auction results. For example, a 1949 Rolex Oyster Perpetual model with a cloisonné enamel dial sold in 2014 at Christie's for $1.2 million. Only in 2005, it had sold for $83k—a phenomenal return. Clearly, such record-breaking results are by no means representative. As with stocks, there are always outliers. However, the thing to keep in mind here is that, there are still many extraordinary investment pieces out there that can improve the above-mentioned return expectations by a lot. So in order to manage your expectations: if you calculate with a 5-6 percent target return at a very low volatility and see everything else then as additional upside optionality, that's probably a good starting point.

Tax Efficiency

Depending on your country of residence and individual circumstances, your returns on watch investments might be free of capital gains tax and other taxes. While taxes are a complex and evolving matter in many jurisdictions this is often the base case for investments in wasting assets. In countries where vintage watches are classified as wasting assets by government authorities, this means that any profits made on the sale are not subject to capital gains tax. This fact alone makes the addition of watches to a personal investment portfolio a sound idea, especially in high-tax jurisdictions. The underlying reason behind why and how gains from vintage watches are not taxed due to their nature as wasting assets differs by country and you should assure yourself and consult your tax advisor first before acting blindly.

Non-Pecuniary Dividends

By now you know already about the most important investment highlights of watches. The points we mentioned so far together form the basis of why investors should add watches to their personal portfolio. Then, of course, there is another side to this. It is the emotional draw that makes this very special asset class different from other assets. As mentioned earlier, passion investments offer *non-pecuniary dividends*. Aside from benefits such as capital gains and diversification, investors also appreciate enjoyment and pride in their investment—a phenomenon discovered by a team around London Business School professor Elroy Dimson while examining the performance of wine, another passion investment.

Moreover, watches and the level of artisanship associated with fine watchmaking can bring people together. Unless you always carry your favorite artworks by Gerhard Richter with you or leave your 1968 Ferrari 330 GTC or Porsche 993 Turbo key on the meeting table, a piece of high horology carried on your wrist at an important meeting carries a much higher probability of being a positive conversation starter than any other passion asset. New friendships will be made, and similar passions might be discovered. In the end you can, of course, try to direct

52

a conversation towards your passion for rare Japanese whiskeys, but simply wearing your vintage Patek Philippe chronograph from time to time can be a very different proposition.

Watch Market Dynamics

"The vintage watch market has become as established as those for art and automobiles, and thus it's become a similarly sustainable alternative investment."

– Aurel Bacs (Bloomberg, 2018)

The Resurgence of Vintage

When I visited the Patek Philippe Art of Watches Grand Exhibition in New York City a few years ago, I was blown away by the crowd there. It had been several years since I had been to a similar event in Manhattan, and I was honestly not expecting an eclectic line-up like that. The attending crowd was an unusually vivid mix, very different from what I expected. Everyone was there—SoHo hipsters, eclectic entrepreneurs, mid-town financiers. Inside, I struggled in the beginning to make it into the most sought-after room: the room of pre-owned watches that had been worn by famous American politicians, businesspeople and artists. The sheer mass of enthusiasts across all ages, especially many younger ones—who would easily fall into the millennial category—streaming into this room struck me. It was synonymous with a development that can be seen clearly worldwide: the unstoppable growing interest in vintage watches and a new crowd of enthusiast investors and collectors emerging.

Later that day, while having a Martini at the 1 Hotel in Brooklyn, I discussed this development with a good friend of mine who is an associate professor in psychology. According to him, one way to explain this resurgence of the vintage watch market is that millennials, and to a lesser extent the Generation X one decade before, have been raised in an increasingly digitalized world. At the same time there has been a lot of focus on retro. Everything seems to be retro, from fashion to accessories to tech equipment. Whether we are looking at cars like the Fiat 500, Charles Eames inspired chairs or digital mirrorless cameras that look like a Leica M from the 1970s the retro wave plays a massive part in our world today, which doesn't leave the watch world unaffected.

Watch manufacturers, meanwhile, have jumped on that train and are releasing one heritage-, tribute-, or re-edition after another. The sheer omnipresence of romantic nostalgia has also had a massive effect on the level of demand for rare mechanical timepieces. In addition to being captivated by the vintage theme, the new generation of watch investors and collectors has for the first time a unique advantage: no longer do they need to rely exclusively on the advice of a secretive group of *supercollectors*. In the age of high-quality online and affordable second-hand print resources, they have instead an immense amount of highest quality information immediately at their fingertips, most of it wherever they go. This unstoppable development has leveled the playing field for the vintage watch world and is not going to end anytime soon. For the millennials in their mid-thirties that I saw in the aforementioned Patek Philippe room in Manhattan, the essence of style in the 2020s is wearing a unique vintage timepiece while still reading the time from their state-of-the-art smartphones. The interest in vintage watches is a way to give their lives a tiny bit more soul in an increasingly digital and sometimes cold world.

Timepieces are not the only means to express such desire. For some it is watches, for others it is classic cars. In a world where semi-autonomous futuristic electric vehicles are soon to take over and near-perfect manufacturing is the norm in this day and age, people are seeking classic cars as a way to breathe—breathe the same spirit, the same story, and enjoy the same feelings as their grandfathers did half a century ago. And this very motive is exactly the same for vintage watches. The once opaque and secretive vintage watch market has been opened, and our information economy is today the ideal platform to ensure it prospers over the years to come.

The impact of digital information on watch investing and collecting is unprecedented in the watch world and has helped to manifest the industry boom over the last decade. New aspiring collectors and investors are able to get a quicker head start now. Just a few years back, the amount of information and availability of documentation was far less excessive. You had to crawl through watch forums, collect old magazines, carry heavy book bands and most importantly attend physical collector meetings to conduct your due diligence. Nowadays, the quality of informational videos on specialist blogs is often mind-blowing and it is no longer comparable to a handful of specialist sources that were available a bit more than a decade ago.

Today's Market Environment for Watches

"There's a stereotype in the world of vintage watches, thanks to a classic cartoon trope. A shady man in a brown trench coat and a hat fit for a gangster approaches you on a street corner. "Wanna buy a watch?" [...] These days, [however] vintage watches have gone corporate."

– Kim Bhasin (Bloomberg, 2018)

Not many investment professionals would have taken you seriously if you told them in the 1980s that in the new millennium money would be well invested in rare watches and returns would easily outperform government bonds, savings accounts, and even most stocks. Just imagine the famous scene from Oliver Stone's legendary *Wall Street* movie; the young Bud Fox recommending Gordon Gecko to put his money in a set of vintage Pateks as an investment? Watches are pleasure purchases. They are status symbols. Money spent, not invested. Aren't they?

Most industry experts consider the early 1990s to be the key period when investing in watches started to slowly take off. Right after the industry as a whole had emerged again from its biggest crisis—the 1970s, when the invention of quartz movements caused the so far most serious threat. Today, estimates for the global market size vary; the sweet spot seems to lie around the $40–50 billion mark, including both vintage, neo-vintage and contemporary models on both the primary and secondary market. The market for vintage watches from the manufacturers Patek Philippe, Rolex, Audemars Piguet, Cartier, and Omega is thereby estimated to make up more than $10 billion. According to our estimates, there are today about 1,000–1,500 serious serial buyers for super-high-end vintage watches (albeit this number is rapidly increasing) and I count around 50 reputable super high-end dealers in this niche market.

If you want to draw a comparison to financial markets, there is a strong resemblance to the high-yield corporate bond market in the 1980s. Put differently, we are clearly talking about a niche market that is still in its infancy. For a long time, the second-hand market in particular was only small and had all the characteristics of a true niche market with a highly fragmented base of sellers and buyers spread across different locations. Recent advancements in technology (marketplaces and payment technology) have transformed this market, though, and made it increasingly more digital.

Established collectors were dominating this market for years, but over the last decade or so, better and better educated investors and collectors with deep pockets have emerged in other parts of the world. In the beginning, the watch market was controlled mainly by wealthy European buyers, followed by American buyers some years later. It is rather recent history that so many Asian, especially Chinese, and Russian buyers have gained prominence, especially in the global auction market.

If you are looking at major physical auctions, globalization cannot be denied. At the very first auctions I attended more than two decades ago, there were around three dozen people attending in-person, accompanied by a bunch of telephone bidders. The crowd was international but overwhelmingly from Europe and the US, with some collectors from Hong Kong or maybe Singapore. Compared to that picture, today, the population and diversity of buyers interested in vintage watches have virtually exploded. Not only has the audience grown significantly, but so has the degree of sophistication of the buyers. At the same caliber of auctions, you would see today probably close to 500 bidders (offline and online) from 50+ different countries. The new kids on the block would be collectors and investors from Brazil, China, Africa, India, and Russia, many of whom are still at the beginning of their interest in this asset class.

"The vast majority of top buyers now come from Asia, a number of whom are under the age of 30 and are particularly active in the superstar watches category (in the range of USD 3–4 million). For the other price categories, Asia remains the primary region, with a growing interest from millennials

followed by the USA, EU and the Middle East. The shift to digital and online auction formats, accelerated by Covid-19, comes at a time of increased interest from millennials and Generation Z."

(Credit Suisse, 2020)

While many Russian and Asian buyers were in the beginning more interested in contemporary models, it is an increasingly visible trend that this clientele is directing their interest now more and more to the vintage world as their educational progress in watches goes on. While this means more competition and less potential for a bargain of the century, the higher number of market participants also increases the efficiency of the watch market. While this will make steep bargains less and less likely over the years, a larger and more diverse bidder universe creates stability for prices by higher and more predictable, steadier demand and is therefore, in summary, a great development that we should all welcome from an asset class perspective.

Notably, the degree of information and readily available knowledge in the market has helped attract new parties into the vintage watch game. Hybrid dealer-information websites like Hodinkee, A Collected Man, or Theo & Harris go beyond just selling watches and are instrumental in increasing market transparency for a wide range of watch buyers. The result is that today we are looking at the most informed watch investor and collector base that ever existed. The education and sophistication process (which is still ongoing and the reason also for writing this book) has helped to fine-tune the knowledge of many existing players. With the help of collector meetings that are organized via Instagram, online forums, and (back in the day) mailing lists, the once high degree of opaqueness has been removed from the market, and transparency of information has spurred new confidence for buyers. This increased degree of confidence has also turned more collectors over the years into investors. They can say today with higher confidence that their purchase is more than a pleasure purchase and maybe even more than just money well parked—actually a decent investment.

Stakeholders

There are several stakeholders involved in the vintage watch market that one must understand. Given that the asset class operates without a centralized public exchange (such as the New York Stock Exchange, for example) where buyers and sellers come together, the market can be described as over-the-counter (no matter if the transaction then ultimately happens online), meaning private, decentralized transactions characterize it. We will now take a brief look at the key stakeholders that participate in this market.

Collectors

Over the years, I have bought a lot of watches from collectors, probably most of all. I truly admire collectors for the non-financially motivated pursuit of their passion. I have built a network of watch collectors and investor-collector friends and acquaintances over the years and recommend you do so as well. First, start locally. Over the years, you might then slowly increase your reach. Online tools like forums or social media groups are a great way to do so. Instagram, WhatsApp and YouTube are strong contenders that have started to gain more and more prominence. Even if you aren't a millennial, and you don't feel like posting your holiday pictures on social media, you should definitely consider opening an Instagram account dedicated to your watch passion and your investments. My networking with collectors didn't happen overnight, but it enabled me over time to see stunning collections, conduct research, build trust and then—at the right point in time—also get that so important very first call to buy a certain piece my collector decided to sell—sometimes even at a discount to its fair value.

Wait a second. A collector selling at a discount—why would that happen? Buying from collectors has a special appeal because they often act more emotionally and—albeit never stupid—are less financially driven. If that sounds harsh, it is not intended to be. As mentioned, collectors have an admirable motive. But when the taste of one of my collector friends changes and they have a new "project" in mind—a term that watch collectors like to use for their next planned purchase—time can be of the essence and pressing them to release funds to conduct their next purchase. Many don't want to think about the financial merits of a then necessary transaction in detail and are willing to sell at a price that is not representative of the money they would achieve, say in an auction three months from now. Often the sale price is then at a discount to the long-term intrinsic value, which could only be realized months down the road—a period often too long to wait for the pressed collector (sometimes this even leads to fire-sale prices so low that I decline to accept).

Some of my collector friends I buy from are amongst the smartest and most educated people in the watch world, and, as said, I do truly admire them. But if I can tell you one thing then it is that changes in personal preference or *mood* and irrationality still occur all the time. The financially-driven investor must be positioned (for what he is) and get that first call (or social media notification) when a fire sale is approaching. At times I offer close contacts a buyback guarantee so that they can get their beloved piece back. While this sometimes hurts my returns in the short run, it helps to keep the relationship healthy, which is often even more valuable. Aside from no fees you are also more likely to be able to acquire a curated set of two to three watches (or more) at once when buying from a collector. Often such a precious set has been put together over years and years of collecting, networking and research. Such sets can be of much more special importance than just one watch alone and increase the *sum-of-the-parts* value significantly.

Dealers

Call me old-school, but I still love an independent dealer with a physical store. I love to discuss inventory and develop a relationship with the dealer face-to-face. Fortunately, there are more specialized watch dealers all over the world than ever and their number is steady or growing—a rarity in retail.

Dealers can vary from multi-store dealers that have their network across global metropoles to more traditional single shop dealers where the business sometimes is family heritage. Moreover, there are also many pure online dealers nowadays. Over the past couple of years, broker-dealer platforms such as Chronext or Watchfinder have become strong players, and generalist secondhand platforms aside from eBay such as TheRealReal, StockX or Vestaire Collective are also offering a growing selection of watches (predominantly contemporary and neo-vintage). Here, one specialty of the watch market is the high level of information asymmetry arising from a unique market composition: while ca. 95 percent of sellers in the secondary market are professional or semi-professional, the same percentage of buyers are retail buyers.

Speaking of dealers, you heard it countless times before: you are always buying the dealer first. Buying from dealers has several advantages over buying from private individuals. Dealers, online or offline, usually give some warranty or guarantee (depending mainly on the local legal framework) for the watch and usually it's permitted to return the watch (if acquired online). This gives buyers additional security. However, buying from a recognized dealer almost always comes at a premium. It's not that they want to trick you; it's simply the business model. The dealer needs to acquire the watch, authenticate it, carry it as inventory, and make a margin when selling it to you. On top, dealers have to handle the risk arising from the mentioned warranty/guarantee. For that reason I usually try not to sell to a dealer when monetizing a watch without significant time pressure. However, especially at the beginning of your watch investing career, your local vintage dealers will be a major anchor point, and you should try to build a good connection to your local dealer where the assortment suits your investment style and interest the most. The list below shows an inconclusive list of highly trusted and very well-regarded watch dealers globally. It is only a small excerpt and has a skew towards high-end investment-grade watches; however, it will give you a rough idea about reliable tier-1 dealers near your area.

Recommended (Vintage) Watch Dealers

An Incomplete Selection

A Collected Man, London, UK

Amsterdam Vintage Watches, Amsterdam, Netherlands

Ancienne Vintage Gallery, Barcelona, Spain

Andrew Shear (ShearTime), New York

Bonanno Gioielleria, Rome, Italy

Caso Watches, Naples, Italy

Eric Ku (10Past10), Hong Kong

Gruenberg Watches, Los Angeles, USA

Jerome Fellous/Watchmywatch, Paris, France

John Nagayama (Onebehalf), Tokyo, Japan

Matthew Bain, Miami, USA

Maurizio De Angelis, Pisa, Italy

Meertz World of Time, Munich, Germany

Momentum Dubai (Tariq Malik), Dubai, UAE

Monaco Legend, Monte-Carlo, Monaco

MMC Montres Modernes et de Collection, Paris, France

Onlyvintage, Monte-Carlo, Monaco

Roberto Randazzo (Newoldtime), London, UK

Shreve, Crump & Low, Boston, USA

The Keystone, Los Angeles, USA

Vintage Watches Miami, Miami, USA

WatchAhead, Rottach-Egern, Germany

World Time Belgrade, Serbia

41 Watch, Paris, France

Watch Shows & Exhibitions

At the time of most of this writing, mass gatherings around the world are still canceled for 2021 in light of the ongoing Covid-19 crisis. Nobody still knows where the (watch) world will go exactly in future. Yet, going forward, watch fairs dedicated purely (or mainly) to vintage watches will hopefully remain a vital hunting ground for investors willing to buy or sell watches. At these fairs, dealers and collectors are present with parts of their collections that are for sale. While there is naturally more competition, such events can still be a great opportunity to buy rare pieces and, at times, even whole sets. Some of the most important global watch fairs focused on secondary watches included pre-Covid the Original Miami Beach Antique Show, the International Watch and Jewelry Guild (IWJG) exhibitions in New York, Las Vegas, and Miami, the Frankfurter Uhren- und Schmuckbörse, Top Marques Monaco, the Parma Watch Show, VO Vintage at Vicenzaoro, or the New York Antique Jewelry & Watch Show— to name just a few.

Auction Houses

The most transparent yet usually the most competitive (and expensive) way to buy a watch is via auctions. While traditionally only conducted offline, over the years online auctions have become increasingly more popular and hybrid auctions are nowadays the new norm. Competition in the auction circuit has become fiercer over the last years, and a handful of houses are dominating the market for watches. Watches as an asset category are covered by all the large, integrated auction houses that are also selling art or antiques. Next to the already mentioned Big-4 global houses (i.e. Sotheby's, Christie's, Antiquorum, and Phillips) there are also smaller, more niche auctions run, for example by local dealers such as Monaco Legend or Cambi Aste. It is safe to say that auction houses are your best bet if you intend to acquire some of the world's rarest watches.

However, one thing that surprises many novice investors is that they seem not to recognize that, even for lower-priced models, there are plenty of lots at auctions available. The auction model for watches works very similarly to the art world. While auctions might be somewhat less attractive for pure bargain hunters searching for out-of-favor, deep value pieces, they are perfectly suitable for investors looking for continued future value appreciation and positive price momentum. Two factors drive this: first, only in rare cases will an auction house decide to offer a watch of which they cannot judge the demand in advance (which they cannot always for out-of-favor watches). Hence competition will be rather high at auctions and neglected lots are much rarer than (virtual) paddle fights. Second, there is the buyer's premium to be paid. Buyers pay this premium because certain (very rare) watches are not available through marketplaces other than auctions. Additionally, you get arguably the highest degree of buying security (watches offered at large auctions are pre-examined and tested for condition and authenticity), which is another reason for the premium. But also for sellers, auctions involve an additional layer of fees, the so-called seller commission, making them much more costly for both sides than a privately negotiated deal. However, as a seller, you have the unrivaled advantage being able to approach a very large, yet targeted audience as potential buyers for your timepiece.

The most important auctions for vintage watches, both in terms of the pieces that are put up for sale and the prominence of attendance, are probably the Phillips and Antiquorum auctions in Geneva. In particular, the head auctioneer for watches at Phillips, Aurel Bacs, did a phenomenal job over the last decade of enhancing knowledge among watch collectors and investors across continents, which puts many of his past auctions among the most important watch auctions in history. In October 2017, he famously sold the most expensive Rolex ever, Paul Newman's Rolex Daytona (the YouTube clip of which is a must-watch for any watch enthusiast).

As mentioned, timepieces coming up for auctions are guaranteed to be 100 percent genuine and are verified by a team of experts. They often represent the rarest of the rare watches (you will have a hard time to get, for example, a pristine Patek Philippe Ref. 1518 not via an auction or acquire the occasional Rolex prototype elsewhere). Over the last couple of years, watch auctions have gained significantly in importance and Phillips (in Association with Bacs & Russo) emerged as the dominating force behind the market. But what marks the importance of a watch house? It is its ability to source new pieces to be sold from its clients and, in parallel, curate the best possible field of buyers for a particular watch or category. So-called mega auctions play an important role and have a signaling effect. For example, Phillips recently sold a couple of record-breaking pieces, which are headlines that help the house to keep that momentum of clients and buyers going.

I remember well that when I started taking part in auctions in the early 2000s, Christie's and Sotheby's were still the leading house closely followed by Antiquorum. As with any highly competitive field, there are natural shifts in dominance and poaching between the players. Someday in the future, there might be some natural rotation again. It is not easy for an auction house that has been on a roll to keep up the momentum of sourcing highly valuable timepieces for the next big auctions. Integrated mega auction houses such as Christie's and Sotheby's have recently been somewhat in the shadow of Phillips in terms of mega-auctions. Still, they will remain key players in the field as they have one important advantage over the long run: attracting new affluent first-time buyers into watches. The largest cross-category powerhouses boast a massive brand name and can leverage their existing customers (from departments such as art or jewelry) and bring them into the watch world. Phillips certainly has Aurel Bacs at the moment, but Christie's and Sotheby's have the unrivaled brand image that takes decades to build.

All in all, auction houses remain one of the most important stakeholders in the watch world, and it makes sense to familiarize oneself with them early. Even if only attended passively and without placing bids, auctions are not simply a medium to buy and sell but are the perfect training ground for novice investors looking to get a feel for what separates just "old watches" from vintage masterpieces.

Excursus: Portrait of a Star Auctioneer

For more than the past decade, one man has become the single most significant and influential auctioneer in the watch world and has also helped to reshape the entire vintage-watch culture. Admittedly, the attribute "influential" gets thrown around a lot these days. However, there is only a selective group of people around the globe that truly deserve such a term to be associated with their name, especially in the vintage watch world. Swiss auctioneer Aurel Bacs, who earned his stripes as a watch specialist with Sotheby's, definitely is one of them. He is probably the most important intellectual contributor in the vintage-watch world today, breaking auction record after auction record, and making it a pleasure to watch him at work on the rostrum. His charisma, enthusiasm, and knowledge attract the Who's Who of the watch world to his auctions. His mission over the last decade has been to empower the buyer, whether investor or collector, with knowledge. This stands in stark contrast to the modus operandi that most other high-profile auctioneers and vintage-watch dealers used to practice (and the majority still does). Bacs took a different approach and understood that by giving a broad audience (i.e. you and me) the same access to information as the most sophisticated players in the game have, he would break the invisible knot and expand the appeal of vintage watches permanently. And this is what happened in the watch world over the last few years. Many fellow watch enthusiasts put it right, saying that watching Aurel Bacs perform on the rostrum during the world's most important watch auctions is no less than pure perfection.

Different Types of Investment Watches

Not all investment-grade watches are equal, yet investors always strive for categorization. Once again, it makes sense to borrow definitions from the framework of stock market investors and use the descriptions *"value"* and *"growth"* to classify investment-grade watches—a concept of differentiation first introduced by star collector-investor Alfredo Paramico. While incomplete at best, most investment-grade watches still tend to fall more or less into one of the two categories.

Value – Rare Vintage Watches

Vintage timepieces that fall into the *value* segment comprise watches that are being offered (for example, during an auction) below your reasonable estimate of their long-term intrinsic value. By definition, these timepieces are rare, and their supply is limited as production has ceased. For Rolex, this category includes most certainly the Pump Pusher and Zenith Daytonas as well as early Explorers, among others. For Audemars Piguet, we have the military or old-font D-series 14790s, first-gen Offshores, and maybe Kasparov Chronos in this segment. All of these are prominent, highly investable watches that are still under the radar when compared with the Paul Newman Daytonas or important Submariners. The *value* category also includes so-called out-of-favor pieces, the deep value niche so to say.

But what does value really mean? It is important to remind us that price and value are two distinct components of any investment. While the price is set for a certain transaction at a specific point in time, the intrinsic value is a much more long-term oriented concept and often difficult to determine objectively at any point in time. Temporary differences between the price and the value of a watch occur all the time and for all kinds of reasons. A certain model might, for example, be overlooked or temporarily out-of-favor. A private seller might be in some sort of financial difficulties and forced to sell quickly at a lower price or the geographic reach of the sale or auction might simply not be large enough to attract sufficient demand. A price-value imbalance is a consequence.

Almost by definition value and vintage go hand in hand. During his research and due diligence, the savvy watch investor has to build an informed opinion regarding the value of a timepiece for sale. The devil is in the details. This step is by far the most challenging part and requires vast experience and a rigorous process. In practice, this is done by comparing condition and price to recent auction results, but it also involves having an ear at the market. Of course, it takes time to build the necessary knowledge that a novice investor needs. But you will be surprised how quickly one can get a good feeling for realistic values. It is hard to describe, but the more you study, do research, and look at prices and auction results the quicker you also will develop some sort of gut feeling, or, as I like to call it, "instinct". It's a feeling for models that will (re-)gain in value or will not. In practice, oftentimes, watches that fall into the *value* category might have recently disappointed during a few auctions, maybe because their design or style was less in demand. While arbitrage in certain niches (e.g. stressed sellers or geographical arbitrage) is also possible, the ascent of online information has made it more difficult.

One of my non-Rolex out-of-favor value investments that I traded recently was a set of two pristine Heuer Autavia chronographs Ref. 2446; a reference full of history, which had been out-of-favor for the most part of the early millennium. The brainchild of Jack Heuer no less, this watch was inspired by dashboard timekeepers (AUTomotive) and airplanes (AVIAion) during the 1960s. Undoubtedly, the Jack Heuer era is cherished by collectors and celebrated at auctions in remarkable fashion. It's hard to ignore their staggering performance in the midst of a thriving vintage market.

The Autavia had long been tipped a deep-value bargain among Heuer connoisseurs. When building conviction during my due diligence, it became evident that such a piece full of history and most cherished already by die-hard Heuer collectors was trading at a significant discount to its fair value. To my surprise, there was on top a significant regional difference in demand, and Germany and Austria in particular were the perfect places to hunt for bargains of this reference. Nobody could tell with confidence back then in 2007/08 when this gap between value and price might close again. Still, with the visible focus shift towards *heritage* among many watch houses and the ever-increasing popularity and value of vintage Heuers, it was only a question of time. Recently Autavias across the board then gained significant investor attraction, and I used this uptick in demand to sell with a decent profit—multiple times my initial investment. Autavias are a remarkable example of the staggering performance *value* watches can have amid a thriving vintage market.

To sum up, the art of predicting which models will be future winners but are currently just seeing some clouds hanging over them is both rewarding and challenging. If this still sounds very cryptic to you, do not worry. We will cover throughout the next chapters in detail what exactly makes up the value of a watch.

Growth – Outstanding Contemporary Timepieces

The *growth* segment comprises exceptional, usually contemporary or neo-vintage (i.e. less than 20 years old) watches that have a promising outlook for future value appreciation but might be even still in production. In other words, these are typically much younger models that might be the winners of tomorrow. Usually, such pieces are well-known models that have recently drawn lots of attention, for example with prices at auctions above estimates. Prominent examples are most F.P. Journe models, including the Chronomètre Bleu or the Chronomètre à Resonance lines. F.P. Journe is still a young watch brand that is already in high demand. Consequently, it is incredibly hard, if not impossible, to hunt for a bargain. But on the other hand, it is most likely that the momentum of F.P. Journe will only get faster once the brand starts to attract an even wider audience. Supply is tight and demand might last for the next years and will continue to drive up secondary market prices further. Other examples frequently

71

include limited (yet still broadly available and produced) editions of contemporary watches of hot Tier-2 brands such as the Tudor Hulk Ref. 79230G (only sold in Harrods London) or the numbered (and eventually soon discontinued) Pelagos LHD Ref. 25610TNL. Don't be fooled, though. For contemporary pieces, the tolerance for wear and tear and the expectation of outstanding condition and completeness of the accessories are often even stricter, and mint condition is more important for a watch to qualify as an investment piece. The history of such a *growth* watch is ahead of it, not behind it. Its condition should reflect that accordingly.

We will come to the implications that these categorizations have on the construction of your watch portfolio later. Historically these were two relatively strict camps. More recently, the lines have blurred, and investment limitations of many vintage investors have faded somewhat. Today, I regularly meet former (*value*) vintage-only investors that look now also into the momentum of contemporary (*growth*) models. The truth is that, while the vintage part will likely always remain more important, both watch investments deserve their place and can help an investor diversify a portfolio.

Let us now take a brief look at what the lifecycle of a watch and its journey from contemporary to (neo-)vintage looks like.

Life of a Watch – From Contemporary to (Neo-)Vintage

Every luxury watch runs through its very own lifecycle. Individual dynamics often differ vastly and depend on such things as brand or model. However, over time you will realize that there are recurring patterns and one can generalize the key phases in this lifecycle. While there is no one-size-fits-all, it is important for watch investors to be aware of the typical lifecycle, especially if you intend to invest in watches of all ages.

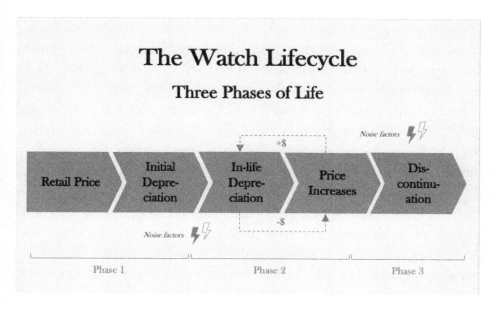

Phase 1: Initial Value & Depreciation – Time spent in the shop window or safe of the authorized dealer waiting for the client marks the first stage of the lifecycle of a brand-new luxury watch. Similar to a car that you purchase new at retail price and move it from the dealer parking lot, a new watch will immediately lose value after the purchase through the first depreciation hit that is erasing the dealer's margin and taxes you paid. Only for a limited handful of hot contemporary models (such as today for the Audemars Piguet Ref. 15202 or the Patek Philippe Ref. 5167A) this is not the case. Supply is kept low and demand so high that secondary market

73

prices surpass the retail price by an "availability premium" that overcompensates for this initial hit. However, one can count the contemporary models with such an atypical price dynamic on a few hands. The vast majority of all other brand-new contemporary luxury watches lose value immediately once you walk out of the dealer's shop and have the stickers removed. During its life, the watch (assuming it is at least sometimes worn) will be subject to a certain degree of wear and tear and will lose more value over time because of the alteration of its original condition.

Phase 2: Life in the Spotlight & Price Increases – Price increases by the manufacturers are somewhat unique to the watch industry as they usually go far beyond inflation adjustment or cost-matching measures. Most manufacturers have a certain price increase rhythm every one to three years. A typical luxury watch might have up to five price increases during its lifetime in the spotlight before it gets either updated or discontinued. Such price increases counteract the value depreciation for secondary market models and can dramatically stabilize used prices.

Phase 3: Discontinuation & Post-Production – As soon as the manufacturer withdraws a certain model from production it enters the discontinuation phase. As no new additional models are released into the market, valuations can start to fluctuate more, and the overall amount of watches in the market will slowly decrease. Ultimately, supply and demand as a function of scarcity will determine the value of your watch now, together with factors such as the current condition and how much it has been affected by deprecation.

Excursus: Noise Factors
Any watch going this typical path is also subject to additional, often completely unexpected influences, so-called unknown noise factors. These are the least predictable factors in a watch's lifetime, and such noise factors differ from model to model. Typical noise factors include generational taste, economic state of the watch's manufacturer, the

production volume and pick up of similar models, interest rate levels, currency effects, special luxury charges and taxes, as well as other factors that are not directly linked to supply and demand of any particular model but relate to spillover effects.

Depending on production volumes, length of the production run, popularity, desirability, and availability, the valuation of a contemporary luxury watch after discontinuation could either increase sharply, continue to plot a similar valuation path or start to decline in value. There are exceptions, but this generalized path gives you a rough indication of what can happen to a watch after the discontinuation of production.

We can look at the Rolex GMT-Master II Ref. 116710LN as an example (the version with an all-black bezel). It was released in 2007 with a retail price of $8,450 as an upgraded version of the previous Ref. 16710. New features included the ceramic bezel, a green GMT hand, a new bracelet and movement, as well as a larger case. During its life in the spotlight, the watch was holding value well but in an unspectacular fashion. Price increases countered the effects of in-life depreciation. In 2019, secondary market values exploded because of two things: first, Rolex announced at Baselworld, the discontinuation of this model (usually, such an announcement gives Rolex sports models a boost in value. And also this time prices jumped by 30+ percent). Secondly, Rolex decided to cease production of the previous Batman on an Oyster bracelet—a noise factor that created unexpected demand for this particular GMT reference (on this very Oyster bracelet).

Part II – Chapter Summary:

- The vintage watch market resurged in the aftermath of the quartz wave and is—despite its tremendous growth trajectory—still a niche market
- Watches as passion asset class boast a range of benefits for investors (safe haven, fungibility, privacy, inefficiency, decorrelation & diversification, capital appreciation, non-pecuniary dividends, tax efficiency)
- The watch market is characterized by a handful of key stakeholders: auction houses, collectors, and dealers
- Investment pieces can be separated in undervalued, exceptional vintage pieces (*value*) and high-price, high-demand contemporary pieces (*growth*)
- Every brand-new luxury watch runs through its very own lifecycle of depreciation and price increases (but patterns exist)

Part III: Investment Criteria

The Secrets of Supercollectors

What determines the value of a watch? What makes a watch precious? What features other than its gold value determine why a particular watch is worth $1,000 and another 20 times that amount? Unsurprisingly, the answer to the question can be as subjective as the question itself. Most watch enthusiasts will answer it with their own spin, depending on their investment or collection focus. In fact, the emotional value quickly comes into play whenever I discuss this question with one of my collector friends. And they are by no means wrong. It is true that for one person it's the Cartier that she inherited from her grandmother, for another is that first Omega that he got for his graduation, and maybe for you it's that Rolex that you bought with your first bonus paycheck.

Emotional value can be a major thing for the owner and can determine its value proposition almost exclusively. However, as watch investors, we need to go one step further. In this chapter, we will try to leave the personal part of the value of a watch aside and isolate the remainder as well as possible. This means we will look at the objective value criteria and characteristics that make up the fair value of a certain watch for an independent third party—an unrelated potential buyer of the watch who does not share the emotional connection and value attribution of the current owner of a given piece. Within that area are we will focus on the most *objective* qualitative criteria that make one watch more valuable than another and the distinct features that have proven over time to let a watch appreciate. But first let us discuss two things:

The Law of Supply and Demand
Like most free markets also the secondary watch market is driven by one of the simplest yet powerful fundamental concepts of economics: the law of supply and demand. Demand in the watch world refers to how strongly a specific model is desired by other investors, collectors, dealers, and luxury consumers. Supply stands for the number of watches that the market can offer. The correlation between price and how much of a good or service is supplied to the market is known as the *supply relationship.* Secondhand prices, therefore, are a reflection of supply and demand. Logically, the fewer examples of a highly sought-after timepiece are available the higher the price. So far, so good—you knew that before. While common sense, the supply relationship is still very important to emphasize and we will come back to it throughout this book, which is why I mention it explicitly.

As a direct consequence, a watch must be considered basically worthless when nobody is interested in it. An extreme theoretical example would be a niche market with few buyers that is suddenly flooded with an unexpectedly high quantity of a particular model. In turn, things look very different when a certain watch is known to exist only five times in the world but 50+ dealers and collectors are eagerly looking to add them to their collection. In both cases, the supply-demand relationship would come out of balance. Hence, when it comes to a public auction in these two cases, prices would reach sky-high valuations, or the watch would not sell at all by failing to reach the starting price.

Condition vs. Rarity

"People are willing to have the best possible watches, originality and condition wise, they are ready to spend a lot for top quality watches but will not move if anything is not correct."
– Virginie Liatard-Roessli (De Griff, 2019)

The two most critical value-determining features of a watch—aside from the brand, which is setting the stage—are its condition and its rarity. Rarity is strongly linked to the supply-and-demand relationship, and we will come back to that in a minute. Let us first get one thing out of the way: the physical condition of a timepiece. Also sometimes described as "quality", the condition is key and of utmost importance. As an investor, you should primarily be seeking pieces in pristine condition. If budget restrictions mean you cannot afford the desired piece in mint, near perfect condition, it is advisable to consider looking for different investment pieces at lower price points. Only in a very few, very special, cases you might sacrifice on condition (like I did at the French flea market). Over the years, I have become much more comfortable paying an at times significant condition premium. I never regretted it. And without a doubt condition will always be of major importance, especially in a market where the assets (i.e. the watches) are structurally getting older and scarcer but the number of market participants (i.e. watch investors and collectors) is becoming larger and larger. Here condition is the single most important and sustainable value driver. Rarity can fluctuate as a function of demand, but the condition is always set and one-directional. Hence, when having to choose one over another, it is clear that it will be condition over rarity for most pieces—assuming the reference is investment-grade in the first place of course.

The growing interest in vintage models will likely lead to even higher demand with steady or even declining supply, in short: a perfect formula for value appreciation. Investment-grade timepieces in pristine condition should stay in high demand and command even more elevated premiums than their less well-maintained counterparts. As you might have guessed, the real value determination process is, however, more complicated than that.

While condition, rarity, and brand are core to every watch investment, what really make the difference are the finer details.

Due Diligence Criteria & Value Drivers

The Perfect Watch

How can you know which watches will make the best investments? What models are most suitable for your portfolio, and which should you avoid? To approach these important questions, we can look outside the watchmaking world for answers. Let us turn our attention to Ferrari, arguably the Patek Philippe of classic cars, the pinnacle in terms of car heritage and performance. Then let me ask you: why is the Ferrari 250 series more sought after than the 330 series? Why are V12 Ferraris so much more in demand? Why are Stradale versions so coveted? The answer is not clear-cut but rather a combination of factors such as production type, number/limited edition, iconic status, technical finesse and even current mood and taste. Ultimately these factors melt together and form the strength of demand, which determines the value of one particular classic car versus another. Similarly, in the watch world, a range of different criteria or value drivers influences valuations and prices.

When determining what price to pay for a certain watch, it boils down to more than a handful of factors to watch out for: brand, provenance, rarity, as well as, of course, again, condition. In this chapter, we will look at these factors and show in detail what drives them. We will also point to the things to look out for during your due diligence process.

We aggregate our findings then into three overlapping areas that are critical for the value of any watch: we call them *Core Value, Mechanical Value,* and *Intrinsic Value.* An immaculate dial, a perfectly maintained movement in pristine condition, and case that is not altered irreversibly by polishing—these points are crucial for the Core Value. The relative rarity of a model and the brand (as a synonym for build quality and heritage) drive the Intrinsic Value of a watch. Its movement and horological complications are most important for the Mechanical Value of a watch. Let us examine these factors now in more detail one by one.

The Value Triangle
Value Drivers for Investment-grade Timepieces

Core

Mechanical

Intrinstic

I like to work with a simple checklist to deconstruct the value of a watch as objectively as possible and leave emotions out of play. I use specific checklists for virtually all my investments and sticking to one also helped me with my investments in watches. I was originally inspired by my friend Reto, a Swiss amateur pilot who I used to fly with sometimes in the past. Even today, with years of experience, he still always works with his checklist ahead of departing with his little Cessna Skylane; he learned to trust it to create and retain his reliable process and avoid errors while flying his small airplane. My personal watch investing checklist is by no means a complete almanac or the ultimate answer, but it helps me a lot going once through it ahead of any potential purchase. In the past, it has successfully helped—similarly to a pilot—to protect me from the worst-case scenario (even if the stakes were obviously far less high than above the clouds) and not get carried away by my emotions when looking at a particular watch.

In reality, my notes are usually much longer, yet less organized. However, I tend to print out this sheet and sit down in silence and think hard before I finally decide to purchase a watch that I am eying. We will work now through the elements of this illustrative checklist step by step in the following chapters. You will find it on the next page as a *preview* of what is to come.

Due Diligence Factors – A Basic Checklist

Model Information			Notes
Brand: Reference: Price:	Audemars Piguet 14790ST (D-Series/MK1) €10,500 (tbd)	Seller:	Reputable private seller (recommended by Armin, long-standing friend of him).
Year:	1992	Type:	Value (neglected mid-size reference)

Value Driver	Due Diligence Factor		Notes
Core Factors	▪ External Condition ▪ Dial ▪ Maintenance Record ▪ Provenance ▪ Case Material	✓ ✓ ✓ ✗ ✗	Condition: external 1.0 (bracelet rather 1.5); movement without issues (2.0); Mint, unpolished case condition, minor signs of wear; no B&P, but service papers, crisp original dial, sharp edges.
Intrinsic/ Intangible Factors	▪ Brand ("Investability") ▪ Model/Reference ("Rarity")	✓ ✓	Old font D-series (Ref 5402-like): traditional 'straight font' logo, reminiscent of early Royal Oaks, long hour mark indices.
Mechanical Factors	▪ Movement ▪ Complications ▪ Unique Features	✓ ✗ ✓	Early MK1's powered by cal. 2125 followed by transition into cal. 2225; Relatively robust and easy to service movement; Watch wears like 38-39mm due to lugs (size sweet spot).
Other Factors	▪ Market Sentiment ▪ Contemporary Production	✓ ✓	5+ yr. waitlist for 15202 (will likely be discontinued soon though), trend towards smaller watches; interesting tropic dial – AP anodized their Ref. 14790 dials to add the blue hue (they did not paint them).
Risks	▪ Seller Reputation ▪ Additional Costs ▪ Liquidity ▪ Externalities	✗ ✓ ✓ ✓	Serviced 6 months ago; Liquidity medium; high demand in Europe; negative interest rates as externality. AP insourcing limiting supply of contemp. models.
Investment Case	▪ Investment Thesis ▪ Time Horizon ▪ Fair Value Estimate ▪ Downside Risks	✓ ✓ ✓ ✗	5+ Years investment horizon, investment case: Tier-2 icon; bet on mean reversion in sizing trends; No bubbly pricing. Fair value ca. +30% higher (closing of value gap to 5402).

Core Value

External Condition

When evaluating a potential new investment watch, several factors need to be considered. Yet, among all these factors, condition—i.e. how well the watch has stood the test of time—is the single most imperative. While some investors seem to have put relative rarity first over the last couple of years, it is a much more subjective matter that cannot make up for external condition over the long run. In the recent past, there has been an increasing demand for all-original, well-preserved pieces—in short, watches in perfect, mint condition—and this tendency will only grow over time. A watch that has been treated with prudence and care is always worth significantly more than a watch that has been beaten down by its previous owner. While this might seem logical, too often I have seen inexperienced watch investors making dramatic tradeoffs when it comes to external condition just to be able to afford a particular reference— unwilling to trade down. Of course, you won't always be able to afford an unworn, absolutely pristine *catalog-style* or *NOS* (new old stock) version of every investment watch you are considering, especially when you are just starting to invest in timepieces. But pristine or mint condition does not necessarily mean automatically unworn or brand new, especially not for 30+-year-old vintage pieces. It means an appropriate relative condition for the age of the watch. "All-original" means here the exact configuration in which the watch has left the factory and was delivered to a client. Hence your main goal should be to avoid heavily polished watches and watches with clear signs of inappropriate wear (such as dirty dials, missing parts, etc.) or even irreparable damage. There are, unfortunately, no fixed rules for categorization of condition and regional differences are present. Still, the condition grades listed below are today generally accepted in most parts of the watch world:

Condition 1 (Mint / Pristine):

- Perfect condition with no signs of wear (if vintage, patina might occur)
- Often comes with all original paperwork and box
- Movement is serviced and keeps time well (+/- 15 seconds a day)
- Bracelet is untouched, all functions and complications work perfectly
- Watch is unpolished with very sharp edges

Condition 2 (Excellent):

- Watch has minor natural signs wear (including faint scratches on case/bracelet), even if only visible under low power magnification
- Last movement service unknown, but still keeps time well (+/- 30 sec.)
- Bracelet usually untouched, all functions and complications work well
- Watch is very slightly polished during OEM service

Condition 3 (Good):

- Watch has normal signs of wear that arise from careful, regular use
- Moderate scratches on case/bracelet or buckle, visible to naked eye
- Watch has been slightly brushed more than once during OEM service
- Last movement service unknown / >5 years ago but keeps time reasonably well (+/-60 sec.), might need regulation or service

Condition 4 (Fair):

- Heavy signs of wear, has been used regularly under harsh conditions
- Deep scratches on the case/bracelet easily visible to the naked eye and watch has several nicks and dings
- Bracelet shows significant wear, has been resized but (but still usable)

- Movement is running but does not keep time well. Functions may not work properly. Not serviced within the previous 5 years (or unknown when). Service (or even minor repairs) needed
- Category rarely accepted by a professional seller/auction house

Condition 5 (Poor):
- Very bad condition, only for spare parts

In most cases the condition grades overlap and need to be split, e.g. by movement, case, bracelet, and dial. While some investors seem to have put relative rarity first over the last couple of years, it is a much more subjective matter that cannot make up for external conditions over the long run. A watch might be worn down, but the bracelet is still in great condition (e.g. it has been replaced early on); hence you will often see mixed ratings and combined grades. It is not unusual that only adjectives (e.g. *mint case, good movement condition)* are used. The adjectives pristine/mint do not necessarily mean the same condition in which the watch left the factory. Natural signs of age (not wear), or patina as we call it in the watch world, are a rather beautiful thing in watches. Minor, natural signs of aging, e.g. through exposure to sunlight, might even enhance the value of the timepiece. Yes, age is beautiful, also in the watch world.

The fastest way to value destruction lies in the misleading thought that polishing or re-brushing the case should be done to remove signs of wear. Especially on the lower end of the vintage watch spectrum, the first thing many dealers do (and customers sadly seem to want) with a newly curated timepiece is give it a good polish, or as I call it *value destruction in action.* Although, more recently, the message got about that by polishing one is irreversibly altering the condition of the watch for the worse, you should be extra careful until the very last dealer out there has understood. As a general rule, watches in original condition are vastly superior to shiny, "freshly restored" watches. A great purchase candidate condition wise would be a timepiece with a case that has never been polished, only has minor signs of wear, a dial that is slightly faded by sunlight, and with luminous indices that have lost their brightness but grown deep and rich in color. Once again, optical patina is often a gift. The movement would ideally have been serviced regularly by the manufacturer.

Yes, that's a lot to ask and hardly always achievable, especially with a limited wallet allocation to your watch portfolio. But the best possible condition is what you should strive for!

Excursus: Polishing – Value Destruction in Action?

A watch without scratches should be better to own than one with clear signs of use, right? Well, not so fast. This is an area where many watch novices make a crucial mistake. If the watch is not an investment and will only ever be worn by yourself and you are a perfectionist that can't stand signs of wear, then things might be different. But for an investment piece, polishing equals value destruction. Okay, minor polishing done by the manufacturer might be acceptable, especially on contemporary pieces. Still, intensive polishing can be a clear and eternal value killer (especially when done by an independent watch-smith without specialist OEM machinery). In fact, on many vintage watch marketplaces, the term "unpolished" is virtually banned, knowing that it is such a hot button. Is the watch over-polished? Does enough surrounding metal stay on the lugs and crown guards? Are the edges sharp? These are the questions to pose yourself to avoid over-polished pieces.

Sure, a scratch-less watch is worth more, but this is only true if it hasn't been polished before. Polishing is a process in which the original condition of the watch is altered by removing a small layer of base material. This cosmetic procedure of turning back the time (in a very wrong way) is not a trend that is unique to the watch investment world. Only two decades ago, when a car collector bought a rare classic car, the first thing he would do right after the sale was some sort of frame-off restoration. Today, a true car connaisseur would hardly touch a restored car like this as an investment. The very opposite is true today. Cars in original condition that show patina and their history are in demand and command a premium. Similarly, naturally scratched and lightly faded classic car interiors are prized at a large premium today, but it took several years for the classic car world to realize this. The story is similar for vintage watches: the watches you buy today in unpolished condition will be worth significantly more and demand a premium.

However, as with every high-value object, profit-driven deception also exists in the vintage world. Watches are not only prone to be replicated but also at risk of being partially faked, i.e. built together or restored with non-original parts. We will pay special attention to this in Part IV of the book.

Excursus: The Condition Report

Whether you buy a watch online or offline, at a reputed dealer or auction, a (vintage) watch should always come with some form of condition report. As a potential buyer your job is to read this report eagle-eyed. There is no standard format, but good dealers do not fall short of details here. Never just skim it or read it only on your phone after being already swayed by the glossy pictures of the timepiece in question. Always stay laser-focused. The oftentimes cryptic language in condition reports demands absolute focus and attention in order to avoid unpleasant surprises. Unfortunately, it is not uncommon among less reputed sellers to try distracting the buyer from inferior features of the timepiece that is being sold, for example by only elaborating extensively on the history of a reference/model instead of describing the condition of the timepiece that is actually being sold. Hence, always read the description very carefully at least a couple of times (and be even more careful if the watch you are looking at seems like an absolute bargain—more often than not there is a reason for it). Look specifically for any wording that might suggest any form of damage (e.g. from oxidization) as well as any indication of swapped or missing parts, dents, chips, etc. Certain features of the watch you want to buy might not be immediately visible in the accompanying pictures but will only be written out in the condition report. A too-short condition report might not necessarily be a red flag. Still, many of the most reputed dealers and all major auction houses understand at least that significant purchases demand detailed information and they provide this in the form of an adequate report.

Dial Condition

The dial makes up one of the most crucial, present, and oftentimes history-laden parts of a watch and deserves utmost attention when considering a watch as a potential investment. It is no less than the *lynchpin* of any investment watch. Overall condition, genuineness, special features (occurring naturally or right out of production), and the amount of possible retouching are key points to look for in any watch dial. Above all, you have to look for authenticity. The million-dollar question is whether the dial is authentic. Everything else comes after.

Again, when buying online from private sellers or less reputable dealers, pay particular attention to the depth of detail that the seller uses to describe the watch dial in the condition report. The amount of information that is disclosed and how detailed the seller portrays this centerpiece of information says a lot about the actual condition of the dial. The dial is naturally one of the first things people spot in the real world and focus on when noticing a watch, e.g. of a new business contact. It should be unsurprising that in the watch investment market, the dial, in particular its condition and authenticity, is at the very center of attention.

To understand this, let us take a brief look into the past of the dial and its historical role. In the first half of the last century, many Swiss watchmakers cooperated as a way to overcome their financial struggles and shared large parts of the supply chain. Consequently, different brands ended up with many identical parts in their timepieces, e.g. for movements, straps, or crowns. Hence, it was ultimately up to the dial to feature the brand identity and draw the customer to a particular watchmaking house. The dial was by far the most important criterion of distinction. Different case shapes, materials, and designs only started to take a more prominent role in the late 1960s and early 1970s when manufacturers became more adventurous in their designs.

Today, most or at least a significant part of the value of a watch rests on the dial, a part that has, however, never been intended to last forever. Naturally aged dials are not only a beautiful thing, they are also increasingly seen as proof of authenticity of a vintage timepiece. While the relationship between patina and partial restoration can be a complicated one, today, this centerpiece of attention is of more enormous importance than ever to the vintage watch market, and it is crucial to exercise vigilance when examining small distinctions. Original watches with near-perfect or unique dials can easily demand a hefty premium over watches that are otherwise 99 percent identical. As such dials play a key role in the *Core Value* of any vintage watch. Seemingly tiny differences such as a retailer signature (e.g. Tiffany, Beyer or Cartier), the stamp of a certain military regiment, a logo of a royal dynasty or just some rarely used colors (e.g. blue dial elements), or unique hands that have been used only for several batches can command dramatic premia.

Timepieces with unique dial features are often highly investable, primarily—once again—due to the law of supply and demand. *Unique* is not necessarily the same as *limited* (although low production numbers are often a contributing reason to the uniqueness). A unique watch is very rare. Still, you must not take the word unique in its most literal sense but rather as an indicator of solitary characteristics that are attributable only to a very small number of watches. In other words, unique shall indicate a mixture, a mélange of different, rare and original. And as we know: different can mean very valuable in the world of vintage watches. One-off or limited production runs, a set of prototypes, uncommon prints on the dial, special hands, different markers, retailer markings, minor optical production mistakes, special issuances for certain companies, military squads or royal families are examples of unique pieces.

Special Dials & Lucky Errors

Special dials can command a significant premium, and it can make a huge difference whether a certain timepiece falls into the prime investment-grade category or is just a nice but borderline investment-grade watch. Consider, for example, the Rolex Daytona Ref. 6263. Why would one watch be priced at say $75,000 and an otherwise identical watch at a 100 percent markup? Same external condition; same owner; same movement, etc. The easy answer in this case would be the so-called Paul Newman *Exotic* dial, consisting of a bunch of squares and contrasting fields of paint. Such features can significantly increase the value. It is due to a change in production that occurred over a very short time and resulted in only a few watches with such dial features.

"It is worth noting, however, that things weren't always this way. Watches such as the Ref. 6263 Daytona—which are now blue-chip, investment-grade timepieces—were once regarded as far less desirable than other Rolex offerings like the so-called 'Bubbleback' references that were especially popular throughout the late 1980s and 1990s."

(Christie's, 2019)

Or consider the Heuer Autavia Ref. 1163. Why can the slightly different Jo Siffert version demand a hefty 500 percent premium over a model that is otherwise identical in condition and specification? Yes, again it's all about the dial. Another example would be the highly investable Heuer Monaco Ref. 1133B Steve McQueen. As it's often redialed, only investors who do their homework realize that the original orientation of the applied indices was horizontal. The radial placement of these elements or vertical orientation would command a significant discount to the horizontal model—a fine, easily overlooked difference that is worth thousands of dollars. Or consider the Audemars Piguet Ref. 14790ST, already a magnificent entry-level investment piece with all the essential features of the significantly more expensive first Royal Oak, the Ref. 5402. Only a certain set of models, produced in the early '90s under the D-series, however, features the original, old original Audemars Piguet font that is also characteristic of the iconic Ref. 5402. These D-series old-font models trade at a premium to their new-font counterparts, which might only be a couple of weeks older and have no differences at all—other than the font of the brand name. The list goes on and on. Just look at Rolex. There are the Cartier and Tiffany dials, the Reds, the double reds, and obviously the mightly COMEX dials. And then there are what I call the *lucky error* dials. The range of special features would easily fill another book. Rolex is clearly also the king of dial variations. Extensive dial decorations such as guillotine or emaille dials or special color dials can be value-enhancing as well. Here the uniqueness factor certainly plays a role, but generally speaking, a model that boasts extensive manual decoration of its dial usually demands a higher price tag and, ceteris paribus, is slightly more investable.

So what are the lucky errors then? In the first part of the 20th century, production processes were not yet as advanced as today, and deviations from the production process were much more common, leading for example to the *crazed* or *spider* Rolex dials. Such error dials today command significant premia and are another sign of the counterintuitive dynamics of the watch market. You will learn about all of them as you move along with your journey as a watch investor.

Consider for example, the classic Rolex COMEX Sea-dwellers and Submariners. These are in fact just very regular Rolex diving watches; however, they were issued to a small number of divers for the French commercial diving company Compagnie Maritime d'Expertises (COMEX); the company logo is printed on the dial. COMEX asked Rolex a couple of times and across references for a set of watches that could plunge down to extreme depths, handle pressurized chambers, and overcome ensuing decompression periods and the watches were never publicly available for sale. As you might imagine, their uniqueness and non-availability to the public, coupled with an extremely low production run, make these COMEX pieces some of the most coveted vintage Rolex watches in the watch world. Other examples of recent record results by highly unique pieces include the quite unusual and unique white gold prototype Rolex Submariner sold by Christie's in 2017 for $628k or the very atypical white gold Rolex Daytona Ref. 6265 sold by Phillips in 2018 ($6 million). Another example is again the legendary Patek Ref. 1518. Only 281 pieces were ever made. The pink dial is a special feature and explains why it commands a much higher price.

I hear you. The titans of watchmaking command eye-watering prices that most of us will never be able to pay for. However, there are also lots of less glamorous examples of watches from Audemars Piguet to Zenith that many investors and collectors likewise overlooked for years (or didn't even know existed). Enter the salmon Royal Oak Ref. 14802ST. Only a batch of the mid-sized Royal Oak watches from Audemars Piguet developed a special salmon-like dial from their originally dark blue dial through natural fading. These natural salmon tropical dials are today highly sought after yet still relatively affordable. And there are much more such unique models than you might think of or that I would ever be able to cover in this book. Just have a look at any of the Geneva auctions in May each year and you will be surprised how many models you hardly ever have heard of will fetch record prices. This is great news for the deep value-oriented bargain hunter in watch investing and a reminder that, even if it got harder, there are still many under-the-radar gems that have not yet gotten the public attention they ultimately deserve. Even the prospect of a potential addition of only one of such pieces to your portfolio should act as enough motivation to always keep looking for the next undiscovered grail. Its tiny nuances that add to the investment value and romance of a timepiece and make them sound investments.

However, such often tiny, hardly noticeable differences also bear a problem. Often the small differences were created more than 50 years ago with relatively primitive methods. They are not akin to a modern-day hologram on a banknote. This opens the market to dishonest sellers. With a small dial swap, they could try to fetch multiples of the normal purchase price. Such a *redialing* is the death knell for collectability. Hence, extensive dial due diligence is of utmost importance to protect your capital. Consequently, you should also dedicate a large portion of your due diligence to the dial. Whether this happens in person or via comparing high-resolution pictures online, it is necessary to do the work ahead of entering the purchase process. This means you have to prepare extensively before looking for a specific model. Once a reference that you target comes to the market, you might not have the time to source the relevant literature and archive pictures in order to conduct proper due diligence. The very best pieces don't remain on the market for ages, and time is often of the essence if you want to secure them. Hence, preparation and research have to be conducted or at last started way before actually looking at objects up for sale. While vast online resources make our investor life significantly easier, they are often absorbed in a rush and the euphoria of an impending purchase does not exactly help to keep the due diligence process as rigorous, cold-blooded, and objective as initially planned.

This is why I want to share some basic guidelines that I developed for myself over the years. They cover the dial examination process that should ideally be adhered to.

A Primer on Dial Due Diligence

The following guidelines on dial examination helped me in the past to stay more focused ahead of and during the purchase process. There are no excuses for the seller not to provide clear, razor-sharp, high-quality images of the dial. If the dial is genuine and the seller has nothing to hide, he will provide them. If not, you should probably look elsewhere.

In the age of Photoshop and mobile picture editing applications that allow for easy correction of optical imperfections, I like to take special care when dealing with new sellers for the first time (remember, you always buy the seller first!). Further into the examination process, you should ask for additional pictures where the watch is set to a certain time that you choose (this way you also avoid a seller using pictures from an earlier sale, something that happens quite often). Even if the watch has only been worn a few times in between two sales, there might be a few additional changes.

As part of the due diligence preparation, any watch buyer should also invest in the required literature or at least have the relevant specialist websites bookmarked. Dedicated book bands with large, high-quality photos of flawless watch models can be acquired online or in specialty watch shops. Many of them are published with the help of famous star collectors such as Auro Montanari, aka John Goldberger, or Guido Mondani, sometimes even with the help of the respective museums of the brand. The most relevant literature comes typically with a rather hefty price tag, but resale values are usually very stable, and these books will save you real money in the long-term. You can absolutely look for secondhand editions, if you don't want to go for all-new editions you can look for well-maintained ones on Amazon, eBay or your local watch shops. You can acquire them step by step and should keep your resources up to date with the most authoritative and well-regarded ones (I have compiled a small list of suggested book bands in Part IV). You will use these books as visual comparison and thereby determine the quality (and value or applicable discount) of your potential investment.

We will cover the due diligence process in detail in a few minutes. Still, it cannot be said too early that you have to learn to pay special attention to the quality and size of the font in texts, differences in serif, as well as special features such as degradation tendencies. In person, use a high-zoom (>8x) loupe and a powerful light and inspect the dial vigorously. If you are looking at a timepiece that is not in perfect condition don't be surprised to find minor dirt spots on older dials or to see natural tarnishing from the silver ingredients in dials through their reaction with water. Also, pay attention to dials that are in too-good-to-be-true condition; if the vintage dial is super-crisp and clear, it has more than likely been replaced (which diminishes the value significantly). Here are my guidelines that helped me in the past, especially for vintage watches.

Excursus: Dial Examination – Things to Watch Out For

- *Printed parts: include, for example, the famous "Swiss Made" signature or other hash marks. These elements are usually not hand-painted, but a stamping/printing machine is used. Markers should be relatively clean and uniform, even if manufacturing processes in the last century weren't on par with today's cleanroom-like standards. Still, expect the variation of the watch model you are examining to be very close to the reference photos. Variation should be minimal. If this is not the case, there is potentially something wrong (redialed or even frankened dial).*

- *(Hand-)Painted parts: have been painted by specialized artisan employees of the watch manufacturers. Naturally, such work cannot have 100 percent precision; however, usually dial painters are highly skilled and have achieved an incredible level of repetition. Hand-painted parts include numerals, indices, markers as well as lumification on hands and indices. What you have to avoid are watches with painted parts that look odd compared to your reference pictures (always bearing in mind that a human has done the painting job). You should e.g. try to spot irregularities in thickness of application or certain parts of the dial that would not have made it through strict quality control (even in the 1970s). If you spot such things, once again better run (or prepare at least to negotiate heavily on price, which usually doesn't work because the seller would rather wait for the next fool). There are obviously exceptions that are less of a deal-breaker. For example re-lumification (especially for dive watches) is usually considered as proper service, and even the most serious collectors will have a much higher acceptance of re-lumed dials. Different luminous materials used in different decades can give you an indication of the age of the dial and whether it fits the rest of the watch (otherwise, we might be talking about service parts). For a vintage Rolex this means, for example, radium was used until the 1960s, followed then by tritium until 1998. Only thereafter LumiNova and newer variations have been used.*

- *Applied parts: these include gemstones such as diamonds, indices/numerals, and the (often raised) corporate logo such as the Greek omega letter or the Rolex crown. Like hand-painted elements, these parts will be added by highly skilled artisans and will run through quality control. Clean execution should be what you expect, and you should look for disqualifying evidence such as wrong alignment or rests of glue visible under magnification that indicate a non-expert has been at work. Also, the alignment of hour indices should be close to perfect, even under magnification.*

- *Case coatings: base finishing is found on most dials other than specially engraved or enamel dials. Such base finishing consists of spray paint or some variation of it. Expect in general a flat and highly consistent color profile with minimal deviations. Ripples, dips, orange peel patterns, and irregular color distribution are often red flags for redialing.*

- *Overall cleanliness: last but not least, take a step back. Zoom out with your loupe and have a look at the overall state of the watch dial and the hands. Rests of paint, oil, glue, fingerprints, or dust are a crystal-clear warning sign for amateur watchmaking, the indifference of the previous owner, or other vicious work that has taken its toll on a dial's genuineness.*

It is never a bad idea to double-check and consult a fellow watch investor or professional watchmaker for a second opinion before finally proceeding with the transaction, online or offline. While dial removal is not always possible, it is often the only way to identify marks on the hidden side of the dial and to analyze overspray or multiple paint swatches that can ultimately unmask even an otherwise nimble redialing effort.

100

Especially when looking at very special pieces that offer the perfect package, this is a step to consider seriously. Ultimately, when you are paying for 100 percent genuineness and pristine condition, you should not be content with a watch that does not live up to this condition.

Maintenance Record

Next to the watch's external condition, obviously, its inner values, i.e. everything related to the movement, are equally important. The heart of a watch cannot have any flaws. Precious timepieces must have been serviced properly and at the right intervals. Similar to a classic Porsche 911 or Jaguar E-Type, not properly adhered-to service intervals for a vintage Patek can start harmlessly and end in a small disaster. While collectors might be able to stomach the follow-on issues that then often arise in the wake of missing service, an investor never should. Once again, especially for your first investment pieces, you might additionally consult an expert to help you examine the inside of a watch. The way I learned to differentiate between various movement conditions was via vintage watch fairs and events, especially in Italy (Parma and Vicenza), which target collectors and investors alike. At such events, you can get a great understanding of what differentiates, for example, a fair movement condition from an impeccable one as you get to see lots and lots of open case backs of vintage timepieces in real life. In an ideal world, you would also always take a deep dive into the service history and review papers and service documents, but especially in the vintage watch segment, complete documentation is an increasingly rare thing. And even if there are documents that come with the watch you are targeting, you must never rely on them solely as even service history documents are nowadays sadly also prone to be forged.

Provenance

"Provenance is what gets me really excited."

– Anish Bhatt aka @watchanish
(A Collected Man, 2019)

Documentation and papers of a watch are not only a way to judge service history; they are also your best way to get an understanding and proof of the so-called *provenance*, i.e. the ownership history of the watch. The best possible scenario would be to buy from first-time owners, albeit such situations are getting increasingly rare and most of the time such watches now come at a hefty premium. First-time owner watches can represent a specific phase in history and—if properly documented—might serve as a time capsule to a certain era , e.g. an IWC B-Uhr of a military commander during WWII or a Benrus DTU-2A/P with certified CIA provenance (as auctioned November 2019 by Phillips) will certainly command a higher prices if provenance is well documented.

History can be documented via the original documents and warranty cards as well as through purchase and service bills. Next to the original bill, it is ideal to have a full history of all trades and changes of ownership of the watch (if possible). Even if it is a challenge, keeping such a record of all watches in the portfolio is something you should strive for.

Excursus: Extreme Provenance
If a watch has documentable provenance of a celebrity, politician, famous businessman or, to a lesser extent, even star collector, this will give the timepiece a significant value boost. Auction results are full of mind-blowing sale price figures for such "extreme provenance" timepieces. Singer and watch enthusiast Eric Clapton's 1987 Patek Philippe Ref. 2499 has been sold for $3.5 million in November 2012. This is a precious and rare model with perpetual calendar and moon phase complications,

however, provenance gave certainly a boost to the achieved auction price.
An even more extreme example for provenance is a fairly basic Omega
Cal. 510 worn by The King, Elvis Presley, which was auctioned for $1.8
million, multiple times what comparable watches achieve. In the fall of
2008, Albert Einstein's wristwatch, a rather discreet, tank-sized Longines
from 1912 has been sold for more than $596k at a New York auction. The
watch was neither particularly rare nor complicated, yet it fetched a price,
usually reserved for the rarest Patek Philippe and Rolex references of this
world. This is what is called extreme provenance. A rich history can add
tremendously to the value of a watch. A prominent owner or strong
connection to a historical event can boost the value of a watch to mind-
blowing heights. There is one watch that has topped it all so far. The
original Paul Newman Daytona. Worn by actor and racing aficionado Paul
Newman, his Rolex Cosmograph Daytona had the inscription "Drive
carefully me". It was a gift from his wife. Phillips has sold the watch in a
2017 auction for $17.8 million, representing almost 20 times the initial
auction lot estimate. Other Daytona references from the same period have
since then benefitted from the Paul Newman hype. For example, a Ref.
6263 Daytona (a model that was recently featured in the box office hit
Crazy Rich Asians by actor Henry Golding) also fetched almost half a
million US dollars. Just the aura of Paul Newman was enough to catapult
the price of these pieces in the air. However, we have to differentiate
provenance from modern ambassadorship where celebrities such a Tiger
Woods are being paid large sums to promote certain brands and models
as part of a wider brand or sponsorship deal. So far this did not have the
same impact as real provenance does (although early Rolex sponsorship
of a certain double-o-agent has certainly contributed to the success of a
diving watch we all know).

However, previous ownership or provenance is not only relevant for
models worn by famous personalities. Generally speaking, any watch with
a fully documented ownership and service history will command a higher

price tag at any given auction or sale process. Obviously, the fewer owners the better (with single-ownership or NOS being the non-plus ultra).

A Word on Box & Papers

Over the last couple of years there has been a tendency in the watch world to put enormous emphasis on the completeness of a watch package or set, in particular the existence of "B&P", the original box and the papers of the watch (i.e. initial warranty card and authenticity documentation as well as the box in which the watch was presented to its first-time buyer, and—if possible—even all purchase and service bills). Watches with such a "full set" usually trade at a 15–20 percent premium (or higher) compared to a watch without box and papers.

Contrary to virtually all other advice out there, I make a case that ceteris paribus—i.e. in the theoretical scenario of having two 100 percent comparable watches to choose from (and crucially: if there is no significant *provenance* involved) for most average investment-grade watches I would always buy the watch *without* box and papers. Yes, you read right. I would virtually always adopt the twin without box and papers. Admittedly, this might be somewhat shocking advice for you. Most watch novices always hear that only completeness of the package can keep the value of a watch intact and, more importantly, can guarantee that you did not purchase a fake or franken watch. This is a fatal yet very common misperception.
I understand if you are confused now. Virtually everything you read online and heard so far put a lot of emphasis on always buying with box and papers. So what's the deal for buying now without them? To answer this, let us deconstruct the B&P mania somewhat and give you an alternative view.

First, the inclusion of the original box and warranty documentation in a watch (without any of the aforementioned provenance features) might give you some initial piece of mind; still, in reality, it says next to nothing at all about the genuineness of your purchased watch. That is not a problem because by reading this book I assume that you have the interest and

104

dedication necessary to be able to differentiate between a genuine watch and a replica very soon. If you follow the advice in this book and keep learning about watches, you will be able to differentiate between, for example, a real Rolex Submariner Ref. 5513 and a replica version with replica movement in a couple of seconds. So the "peace of mind" factor that comes with B&P would become irrelevant anyhow.

Secondly, B&P will not help you with more complicated frankening matters. A piece of paper won't help you to determine whether all hands or the dial are still 100 percent genuine. Instead of relying on the "full set", you must make sure to either become an expert, consult one, or—e.g. as part of an auction or via a renowned dealer—buy from one within your trusted network (see also again our trusted vintage dealer list, introduced in Part II). In fact, I want you to do the work and not trust a piece of paper to guarantee the authenticity of your investment.

This leads us to the next problem that also a full set cannot solve: the vintage watch market is already swamped with replica boxes and fake papers—tendency rising. Yes, you heard right. The replicated item nowadays is more often the box or the documentation than the actual watch. And it's a no-brainer as to why. Let's say we have two identical vintage Rolex sports models for the price of $15,000 with a full set. Let's assume now that the papers for one of the two Rolex watches disappear. This would reduce the value of the watch immediately, and it would trade at a discount of say 20 percent. Hence, a simple Rolex watch box and a piece of paper are worth €3,000 (if they miraculously reappear). And here comes the issue.

"[...] Counterfeiting remains a big issue. According to the Federation of the Swiss Watch Industry, fake watches account for 9% of customs seizures, placing watches second only to textiles as the most counterfeited products. One of the reasons is the internet, as technology makes it easier to buy and sell counterfeit items online."

(Credit Suisse, 2020)

Once you have seen the sophistication of the Eastern European and Asian expert forgers, you will have no doubts that they are able to produce a near-perfect watch box (with no noticeable imperfections) and a perfect copy of the original papers. Yes, the warranty certificates have watermarking on them, but trust me; this is no problem for seasoned forgers in Eastern Europe who produce these certificates when taking a break from forging 500-Euro bills. The fact that technologies have advanced over the years does not help either. While it was very difficult to try forging an original paper from 1981 in exactly that year back then, technology has advanced so much since then that even semi-professional forgers can replicate excellent documentation nowadays.

Even worse is the situation for vintage boxes. Production technology was not perfect in the 1960s, 1970s or 1980s and minor differences were not unusual. In fact, there was no sophisticated forgery back then (and surely not one focused on boxes), which is why firms tended to care less about making sure their papers and boxes were unique and hard to replicate. This causes a problem for vintage buyers today.

In case you are wondering, yes, it is very easy to acquire these fake papers. You no longer have to travel to Kiev or Guangzhou. Today, tons of internet forums and websites sell such forged papers, and I am not even talking about the dark web. Fake B&Ps are easily shipped directly to your door with a couple of clicks and a credit card or PayPal account.

To conclude, boxes and papers are the real low-hanging fruit for forgers and even experts—including myself—struggle to identify the authenticity of a piece of paper, something that they can do relatively easily when looking at the watch itself (and without problem once opening the case back and examining the movement). Things are different if the watch has significant documented provenance, but if not, these are the harsh facts.

Disappearing Premium Theory

Since you picked up this book, you are clearly interested in becoming a watch investor, rather than a purist collector. While there might be an emotional reason that leads a collector to favor a watch with a full set, for an investor, in most cases, there is no such reasoning. The 20-something-percent premium you have to pay for a (potentially forged) piece of paper is not the best way to invest your capital. And here is why: it is fair to assume that the technological advancements over the next years will make it increasingly easier for forgers to replicate vintage watch papers that were originally issued half a century ago. It is less likely that technological advancements on the collector/investor side will develop equally or that it will be easier in the future to identify potential vintage fakes. The natural consequence is that the currently still existing B&P premium will slowly disappear or, at the very least, become smaller over time. For the watch investor, this means that the 20 percent premium might lower to say 10 percent. In this case it is permanently lost money (or at best still a foregone opportunity to generate returns by investing the parked money in another timepiece instead). There are exceptions to this generalization. Very expensive timepieces that have been publicly auctioned by renowned auction houses before, which attested the authenticity of their papers—often via an expensive process that involved manufacturers themselves, conducted by leading experts in the watch world—are exempt from the arguments above. In fact, the very contrary might be true here and the value of these specific sets might increase over time as the number of pieces that get certified in such a way are becoming fewer and fewer. For the average Rolex sports model from the 1980s this is, however, most likely not the case, and I would always rather buy five such watches without papers than four with full documentation.

Case Material

While it sounds straightforward, the material of a watch case (and the bracelet for sports models) can sometimes be a controversial topic. Let us focus first on the case. Today, houses like Hublot or Richard Mille experiment a lot, but traditionally there were only two main material options for vintage pieces: gold or steel. Gold cases could either come in yellow, white, or rose gold. Other variations such as tantalum, DLC coating, or titanium appeared later (and still are) on the market, but over the years, these materials still remained a niche. Aside from some current Rolex-focused price dislocations, brand-new contemporary steel watches are significantly cheaper than their heavy 18-karat-gold counterparts. If storage of wealth is your main motivation for buying a watch, then you could—at least in theory—store a higher portion of value in a full gold watch because of its higher sticker price. But I will tell you why that is not necessarily the best idea and only half of the story.

Historically watch manufacturers produced otherwise identical watches where only the case material was different. For a particular reference, a manufacturer would, for example, produce a certain number of watches in steel then move on to white gold, yellow gold, etc. The number of produced pieces would differ, however. Let's take for example the A. Lange & Söhne Lange 1 line-up. Certain references for Lange 1 models in steel are rarer since most Lange & Söhne timepieces are made out of gold and platinum. Also, in terms of investment returns, there is no evidence that gold watches outperform steel over time, i.e. deliver superior returns; exemplary evidence actually indicates the opposite. This is known as the "steel paradox" and refers to the fact that—albeit being the vastly cheaper material—steel watches can become even in absolute terms more valuable than their gold counterparts, mainly due to their relative rarity.

For many vintage pieces, this is the case because more than half a decade ago, steel was simply not used as frequently for luxury watches. In fact, steel was considered an exotic case material for a luxury dress watch or

108

chronograph in the WWII era. If one watch deserves to be called the "holy grail" for (steel) watch enthusiasts, it is probably the Patek Philippe Ref. 1518 in steel. As one of the most cherished trophy watches in the world today, the steel Ref. 1518 is clearly special, being not only the first but also the only perpetual calendar chronograph produced in such a "cheap" material. In fact, the Ref. 1518 and the already mentioned Ref. 2499 from Patek were the only perpetual calendars with chronographs for the better part of half of the 19th century. Only 281 pieces of the Ref. 1518 were made together counting in all metals—the vast majority in yellow gold, roughly one fifth in rose gold, and only four (so far known) pieces in steel.

So what's the big deal? It might at first glance seem counter-intuitive. Why would simple stainless steel be more desirable than more precious metals? It is here that rarity comes into play and even becomes the dominating factor. As we will learn in the next chapter that aside from its condition, the value of a luxury watch is determined to a large extent by its rarity and there is hardly something rarer than a highly complicated (in fact, the most complicated one for decades) luxury timepiece in steel. Combining the rarity of this metal in the Patek family with the history of this watch's perpetual calendar chronograph—which Patek produced in the middle of the World War II drama—in terms of complication explains why the highest-profile investors and collectors are still desperate to get their hands on this multi-million-dollar piece.

Specific Purpose

Even if you fail to find the next COMEX Sea-dweller or pink dial Patek, you can still focus on *specific purpose watches* that add to a watch's rarity and value. An example would be the so-called pulsation dial manufactured by the likes of Patek Phillippe, Rolex or Longines after World War II in order to help doctors to read a patient's pulse easier. Such features that served a distinct purpose are now highly in demand and can make great investments by acquiring a piece of watchmaking history. If the watch has had a certain purpose, be it a special diver or racing chrono watch, it serves to create a story, which will be key once you want to realize your investment gains. Another example would be the range of Beobachtungsuhren, or B-watches, that goes back to a set of pilot watches of World War II manufactured only by five manufacturers specifically for the German Luftwaffe: A. Lange & Söhne, Laco, Stowa, Wempe and IWC.

Other Factors

Next to the case, also some other parts and factors affect the *Core Value* of a watch. You should normally not turn down an interesting piece because of peripheral parts, such as the bracelet or watchband. A replacement here would affect the value of the watch much less than anything that happens inside the case. But be aware again of counterfeits (enhancing returns by selling a genuine watch case on a replica bracelet is not uncommon among sketchy sellers) and the value reduction implied by a non-original bracelet or clasp. A completely different topic is case monograms. Such case back markings can be another part that influences value. While on a contemporary model a monogram or initials can easily take away a good chunk of value from the watch, this is less so for watches that are more than half a century old (a period where monogramming was much more widespread). On the flip side, there are potentially value-enhancing monograms, especially if they are from high-ranking military commanders, for example, or show some sort of royal provenance.

Mechanical Value

As a watch-investing neophyte, one can easily become too focused on other things and become oblivious to the exceptional technical skillset that is necessary to design, manufacture, and construct the inside of a complicated luxury watch. It is the inner values of a timepiece that make up its *Mechanical Value* for the investor.

A traditional watch is powered either by a mechanical or a quartz movement. The mechanical movement can be either sourced from an external supplier or produced in-house. The company ETA SA Manufacture Horlogère Suisse (ETA), which belongs today to the Swatch Group, has occupied here a unique position in the watchmaking industry since the year 1793. From its production sites, located in the Swiss foothills of Jura and the cantons of Valais and Ticino, today ETA dominates the market for externally supplied movements and has built a near-monopolistic position in supplying manufacturers with external movements. After a consolidation process, the company now also owns the previously independent movement manufacturers Valjoux and Piguet, which gives the publicly-listed Swatch Group, controlled by the Hayek family, an even more dominant position.

Usually, ETA supplies the raw movement (ébauche), which the manufacturer then optically enhances or modifies. In most cases, watch collectors and investors consider a timepiece with an ETA movement inferior to movements developed and manufactured directly by the brand. Since the independent development of an own caliber easily costs upwards of three to five million US dollars, many lower-end brands and low-production niche manufacturers don't want to (or economically cannot) make such large investments and prefer to keep the prices for their models from skyrocketing. However, there are exceptions to this perception and preference of in-house over ETA movements. For example, Tudor's contemporary Black Bay line was originally issued with an ETA

111

movement in a rather small number of pieces. Only a few years later, Tudor moved to an in-house caliber, which is a bit thicker, and made some tiny modifications to the dial. It is not unlikely that these dial modifications, together with the relative rarity and the rather desirable thinness, will ultimately make these early Black Bay ETA models ceteris paribus more precious than their in-house caliber counterparts.

Still, in most cases, an in-house movement is preferred in the watch world. One investor friend once described it to me by saying a feeling of mass-production surrounds ETA movements. A unique caliber, ideally developed solely for a particular watch model or series, marks most of the time a clear driver of value enhancement (and something the majority of your watch investment portfolio should consist of). Even if bare ETA movements are usually enhanced with applications in gold and special decorations, in most cases nothing beats an in-house caliber.

At the bottom of the movement hierarchy remains the quartz technology. In fact, quartz movements interfere with many characteristics that watch investors are looking for. Other than some diamond-decorated contemporary ladies' watches I cannot think of many quartz men's models that I would consider remotely investable (only some Cartier pieces, the Rolex Oysterquartz, and of course, the F.P. Journe Elegante 48 come to mind).

Complications

"Complications (any feature other than the function of telling time) automatically add an extra level of mechanical complexity to a watch, and their inclusion can cause price tags to rise."

– The RealReal (Piters, 2019)

Special technical features, called *complications* in watch lingo, are additional functions implemented in a mechanical watch. For many watch enthusiasts, they are the salt in the soup as they often combine a certain utility in everyday life with craftsmanship and fascination with horological masterpieces. Some technical features are so exclusive and sophisticated that only the best of the best luxury manufacturers are capable of developing and building them. In the vintage watch world, they often mark historical points in watchmaking and are hence one of the cornerstones of watch investing. Thus, it is crucial to be aware of and understand the different kinds of complications and their potential for value appreciation.

Complications are important value drivers and the most sophisticated complications can be a guarantor for future value appreciation. Why is it that complications add so much value to a watch? Who is still using a watch to determine the date or stop the time when one tap on a smartphone can give the same information with much more detail and accuracy? And what is this crazily expensive gimmick called tourbillon? In this chapter, we shall provide the answers to these questions.

Overview of Key Complications

Small timepieces that have mechanical, non-microchip-driven functions are tiny pieces of art and manufacturing finesse. Admirers of that kind of art are willing to pay a significant price. The amount of value that complications can add to a timepiece can be vast. Different complications within an otherwise similar watch will add up and increase the value of a watch. Some of the most valuable timepieces combine for example a chronograph function with an annual calendar. But not every complication has equal value potential for investors. Let us walk now through the different kinds of complications first and then assess their investability.

Chronograph

The chronograph function was initially developed in the 19th century when pocket watches were the first watches that had a mechanical function to stop the time. However, initial versions of the chronograph function were not as sophisticated and required the watch to be reset from scratch after each stopping process.

The breakthrough was achieved by the Austrian watchmaker Thaddäus Winnerl, who in 1831 presented the first chronograph with two overlapping second fingers, a version that was later refined by watchmaker Adolphe Nicole, who introduced the zero-reset function as we know it today. Today the chronograph function is obvious from the two pushers that start/stop and reset the chronograph. A more sophisticated version of the regular chronographs is the so-called flyback function, where a single push of the start/stop button is sufficient to end for instance one lap time and simultaneously start the measurement of the next lap time.

However, the queen of chronograph functions is the so-called Rattrapante version, which loosely translates from French into "catch up". This precious complication starts two chronograph fingers at once. The trailing pointer can be stopped while the second one keeps running, which makes it possible to read interval times. Pushing again will allow the stopped trailing pointer to jump ahead to the still running one. It is a truly

114

remarkable piece of watchmaking art that is also called a split-second chronograph. The Rattrapante function was almost dying in the 1970s when the demand for such complications in watches hit a historical low. Given that production costs were significantly higher due to more complex functions, we are lucky that these functions survived the first wave of electronic watches, back then driven by the emergence of quartz watches. In 1922, Patek Philippe released the first Rattrapante wristwatch chronograph, which around the millennium was sold for over $1.9 million—at that point in time, the highest price for a wristwatch sold at auction. For investors, the exceedingly rare and super-hard-to-manufacture Rattrapante complication remains highly desirable. A few years ago, in 2016, a Rolex Ref. 4113 split-second chronograph was sold by Phillips for $2.3 million, setting a new record for the most expensive Rolex ever sold at auction until then.

In recent years, chronograph complications in vintage models in general have been in very high demand and even mid-tier brands such as Heuer have seen tremendous demand in their racing-inspired vintage chronographs. Maybe it is the sexiness of the world of motorsports that we associate with them, maybe just the fact that this function is actually useful in daily life, or maybe it is just a mechanical fascination. In any case, chronograph complications, and especially the Rattrapante complications, are among the most precious complications and the value of these historically most relevant pieces should only go higher.

Perpetual Calendar

While the name might suggest that the *perpetual* calendar function runs into eternity, such a complication can be found in no mechanical timepiece. Nevertheless, the so-called eternal or perpetual calendar is a highly intelligent complication that uses mechanical finesse to account even for leap years. In fact, this means that the date does not have to be reset every four years, and the calendar consistently knows year, month, date, and even day of the week. The laws of the Gregorian calendar, however, would need this system to be reset on the 29th February 2100.

The perpetual calendar is a highly sought-after complication by watch investors and collectors alike as the mechanical finesse that is required to program a tiny mechanical watch memory so detailed is simply mind-blowing. Only the best of the best manufacturers are able to produce watches with such a complication, which is consequently most often found in watches of the likes of A. Lange & Söhne, Vacheron Constantin and Audemars Piguet. For investors, perpetual calendars are set to remain an absolute value booster.

Minute Repeater

A Minute Repeater is as close to time travel as we can get today. This technical feature of utmost complication indicates the time by a mechanical sound signal: a small hammer hammers against the balance wheel. The house of Brequet was the first to present such a working mechanism. Minute repeaters look back on a long heritage within a range of other watches, more commonly known as *striking watches,* and are considered to be among the most complicated timepieces. Their origins date back the 17th century, when in England the very first striking watches were dumb repeaters, which struck the time on the inside of the case producing a muffled sound, thereby allowing people such as couriers, amongst whom they were popular, to discreetly check the time in their pocket during tedious levees and royal councils without offending their superior by inattention.

Over 100 unique components have to be put together to create this highly complicated mechanism. Decades of the highest possible horological knowledge are required, and the assembly of a minute repeater will easily take more than 200 hours of work. Listen to an old Patek minute repeater today and you will hear the same sound someone heard several decades ago—that's a type of time travel that is enhanced by the effect of sound on memory. The chimes of a minute repeater have the power to remind us of the past and this kind of time travel is highly desirable in every watch investment portfolio.

Tourbillion

The French word for whirlwind plays in the highest league of watch complications, but it does not have much in common with a storm. Rather, the tourbillon is a device used in mechanical watches to improve the movement rate. To do so, it compensates for gravity-induced rate deviations by constantly changing its position. But since it does not add any functions to the watch, very strictly speaking it cannot even be called a complication. Nevertheless, it is an indicator of the high art of horology. Only a few brands have mastered this difficult-to-manufacture horological masterpiece.

Basically, a tourbillon is a cage that houses the balance wheel and its hairspring, the escape wheel, and the anchor. This cage is usually connected to the fourth wheel and is also driven by it. Since the fourth wheel usually rotates 360 degrees once per minute, the tourbillon also completes a full rotation in one minute. This rotation compensates for gear deviations caused by gravity and thus ensures the highest possible accuracy. Therefore tourbillons mark so to say the Olympian standard of watchmaking. While the tourbillon was originally developed for pocket watches, it made sense then. Today, it is rather a gimmick as it is less needed to counter the effects of gravity in a wristwatch. A watch may even feature a double, triple or quadruple tourbillon—the higher the number the more complicated and the more valuable is the timepiece in question for collectors and investors alike.

Alternative Time Zone

In the 1950s, the management of famous former airline PanAm had a special ask of Rolex founder Hans Wilsdorf. Would it not be possible to develop a watch that would allow its airline pilots to be able to read a second time zone while still seeing the main time zone when flying? Rolex promptly answered and released its famous GMT (Ref. 6542). Globetrotters as well as investors and collectors all over the world today still appreciate the value of this second time zone. The Rolex GMT has been the standing model for several other manufacturers that use the bezel to add a second 24-hour wheel to adjust for a second time zone.

Meanwhile, other manufacturers have come up with different solutions for a second time zone. Patek Philippe, for example, integrated a self-winding 24-hour ring in the dial of its Worldtimer (Ref. 5110) on which the names of capitals in different time zones are placed. To know the time in New York or Zurich, the owner of this masterpiece only has to look at the respective ring. Another version of this complication is offered by ultra-niche manufacturer Maison Ciribelli, based on Monte-Carlo. In their Dual Time model line, the last designs by legendary Royal Oak and Nautilus father Gerald Genta, the niche manufacturer uses two watch modules in one case that are running quasi in parallel and are controlled by a single pusher to power two time zones. Time zone functions are not as complicated as other mechanical features, and typically there is—if at all— only a slight value premium attributable to the complication itself.

Other Complications

Of all complications, the moon phase is one of the most impressive, yet least complicated ones. What might look complicated for watch novices at first glance is far away from the finesse of a minute repeater or perpetual calendar. The moon phase complication usually can be boiled down to a simple blue, decorated plate and two moons mounted on a gear wheel with 59 teeth. There are more sophisticated versions (such as some of the IWC and A. Lange & Söhne moon phase mechanisms) and less accurate and complicated ones. Last but not the least, there is the alarm function. Even decades before the first Casio watch, there were mechanical watches that had a built-in alarm clock. The first models appeared in the 1920s and LeCoultre presented in the year 1929 the first version of its wristwatch alarm clock. While early versions were not particularly pleasant to listen to as the sound was rather metallic and often too low to wake anybody up, the famous JLC Memovox has set a new standard for this complication in the 1950s.

Intrinsic Value

We already learned about the external and mechanical value drivers of an investment-grade watch. Now we will finally come to the least visible part, the part of the iceberg floating below the surface: the *Intrinsic Value* of a watch. What might sound somewhat esoteric simply comprises softer factors such as the *brand* and goes on to other qualities such as *rarity*, elements that make up an important role in the overall value framework.

Manufacturer

The manufacturer or the *brand* of a watch is synonymous with heritage and quality and is among the principal value drivers of any watch. The long-standing tradition and craftsmanship of the best of all manufacturers have been honed over decades and serve today as entry-barriers for new kids on the block (this is also the reason why very few new elite brands come to the surface). To arrive quickly at decades of tradition and the sort of skill that houses like Patek Philippe or Rolex have developed is virtually impossible for new entrants in this market. Emerging independent high horology brands that do surface are usually spin-offs (Laurent Ferrier) or are backed by (or working with) star designers such as Gerald Genta (Maison Ciribelli) or Jörg Hysek (Hysek). This makes the brand one of the most obvious but also the most important screening criterion and value driver. This point is so important that we dedicate a whole section of this book to the major brands and rank them according to their investability (Part IV). You will quickly discover that and why Patek Philippe and Rolex are the twin-titans of the watch investing world. The level of recognition that these two brands command, the longevity of their designs and style, and the resulting iconic landmark status of many of their most collectible watches, keep pushing their status (and prices) further and further in the air. Throw in Audemars Piguet and Vacheron Constantin, and you have two more brands that, together with Patek Philippe form the *holy trinity* of watchmaking. These three super prestigious brands all can look back to a very long history, with Vacheron Constantin dating back to 1755. Each of the three trinity members boasts a core collection dedicated to intricate complications, ranging from perpetual calendars and minute repeaters to split-seconds flyback chronographs. Both Vacheron Constantin and Patek Phillippe held at different points of time the "most complicated" watch of the world in their repertoire. Moreover, next to pure mechanics and complications all of the trinity members are using hand-finished movements making use of traditional techniques, including the famed Côtes de Genève—aka Geneva Stripes. Utmost attention is not only given to the visible elements (such as the dial), but also the invisible ones (such as the movement). In case you are wondering why Rolex is not part of the holy trinity, the reason is its different focus and positioning. Rolex focused always on producing the most durable, high-quality timepieces for extreme conditions that are also practical for everyday wear. Fine movement decorations and high horology have never been Rolex's USP. So although current trends and auction prices would speak for Rolex and Patek Philippe leading the field, history cannot be erased, and the term holy trinity is probably set in stone for the unforeseeable future. However, there are many other brands with serious investment potential and in particular certain models of the inventors of watchmaking as we know it today such as Breguet (first tourbillion) and Longines (first chronograph) could also be high up on your watchlist next to some other great independent watchmaking brands such as F.P. Journe or Laurent Ferrier. Moreover, with the supply of vintage watches being in decline and prices on the rise, you might even open yourself to watch brands that are not found being displayed in high street shops around the world. Brands that boast a long history in the watch world but are often unheard of for the broader public. Looking into now-defunct brands, such as Universal Genève or Enicar can be a great way to avoid the often scarily high entry costs of investing in rare pieces of Patek Philippe & Co. However, one thing is clear: as an investor, it is important to resist the temptation to go for lower-tier or fashion brands with virtually no *intrinsic value*, just because they seem more attainable or might be all over your social media ads.

Overview of Key Brands

So why is there so much buzz around the landmark brands, and why should you rather not touch others as an investment? Let us shed some light on this. The manufacturer is of such utmost importance for two reasons. First, manufacturers own brands that represent a certain, oftentimes well-documented standard of *manufacturing quality* and craftsmanship. It is not only commonplace in the watch world that manufacturers such as Patek Philippe or Vacheron Constantin represent the highest level of craftsmanship that can be reached, but these brands can and do prove it throughout their collection. Secondly, it is the *inimitable tradition* and monumental position in the history of watches of certain manufacturers that add to the special value of the timepieces produced by them. Brands such as Audemars Piguet or Patek Philippe also serve as more than just a yardstick for the quality standard of a timepiece. A brand is a sign of heritage, something which has been developed over hundreds of years and cannot be easily replicated. Rolex, for example, has profited not only from being the watch of choice for James Bond or the famous COMEX squad in the 1960s but has also quickly gained a reputation for being the first sports watch climbing the highest mountain on earth, Mount Everest. Hence, the brand is of paramount importance as it breathes and stands for a range of untouchable accomplishments.

Dead Brands Walking

Novice investors often tend to focus exclusively on brands they knew or liked before they started to develop a deeper interest in the asset class. If the budget is limited, this can be a mistake. Don't ever write off a brand, just because it didn't present a new model at the latest Watches & Wonders exhibition or it does not showcase their watches next to the usual suspects in the luxury department of a super watch store in London or New York. Many highly investable vintage models are from brands that had glorious times in the past but are either dormant today, or even have already completely disappeared. A striking example of a dormant brand today would be Longines. The Swatch-owned house nowadays is an entry-level watch brand without much special character or immense prestige in their contemporary line-up. Yet, the almost 200-year old company occupies a unique position as one of the inventors of the chronograph function in watch history and their vintage chronographs are highly sought after by high-profile investors and collectors. The fact that the company's current contemporary models aren't highly regarded by the watch world does not affect its history as one of the founding brands of watchmaking as we know it. Hence, the current production line of a brand must sometimes be completely separated from a brand's historical products. An even more extreme example would be Universal Genève. The brand has ceased to exist since the 90s, but still fetches impressive prices at vintage auctions, and has produced a range of remarkable investment pieces.

The Investability Pyramid

The investability of a watch brand can be shown via a pyramid structure where the most renowned, best-in-class watchmakers offer the safest and best route to value appreciation.

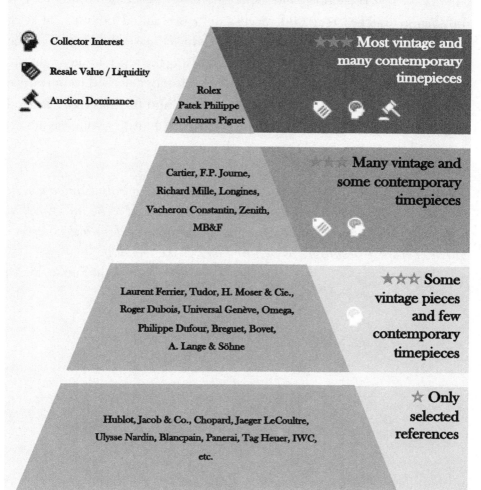

The Watch Investability Pyramid
Illustrative Classification of Watch Brands

Collector Interest

Resale Value / Liquidity

Auction Dominance

★★★ Most vintage and many contemporary timepieces

Rolex
Patek Philippe
Audemars Piguet

★★★ Many vintage and some contemporary timepieces

Cartier, F.P. Journe,
Richard Mille, Longines,
Vacheron Constantin, Zenith,
MB&F

★★★ Some vintage pieces and few contemporary timepieces

Laurent Ferrier, Tudor, H. Moser & Cie.,
Roger Dubois, Universal Genève, Omega,
Philippe Dufour, Breguet, Bovet,
A. Lange & Söhne

★ Only selected references

Hublot, Jacob & Co., Chopard, Jaeger LeCoultre,
Ulysse Nardin, Blancpain, Panerai, Tag Heuer, IWC,
etc.

Here you find a non-exhaustive ranking of investability, obviously illustrative and subject to many exceptions. While it might sound obvious that rare pieces of the likes of Rolex and Patek Philippe are predestined to appreciate, novice investors often focus too early on finding a diamond in the rough or are distracted by brands of low investment-grade with high marketing budgets that occupy high street watch shops with their contemporary models.

Limited Editions & Low Production Models

The basic law of supply and demand is key when it comes to low production watches (<20,000 pieces) or truly limited editions (at least <5,000 pieces, better <1,000). I had to introduce the word *truly* since some watch manufacturers have and are still overusing the term "limited edition" and have tried with virtually every other watch they released to introduce some perceived rarity. Whenever you find a brand that has more limited than regular production models, be careful with your assumed implications on value arising from such "limitation".

"Vintage timepieces that are out of production or inherently limited can be a good investment, although collectors ultimately tend to be motivated by fascination and passion when they acquire a rare, hard-to-find timepiece to either display or admire as part of a lucrative collection."

(Credit Suisse, 2020)

Excursus: It's a Man's World

Watch investors primarily look at men's watches. Ladies' watches are usually considered less investable (and less collectible) and hold their value much worse. The underlying reason is not a gender question but is a matter of size. Given the smaller dimension required to fit a ladies' wrist, manufacturers simply cannot use the same technical complications and finesse in a smaller ladies' model. That is not the only reason, but my investment advice is in general to stick to men's watches, even if ladies models often seem to have superior case features such as diamonds and appear to have lots of Core Value. Especially in the 1940s to 1960s, miniaturization technology for watches was still in its infancy, and ladies' watches consequently were less complicated. If you are a woman (or want or need to add a few female watches to your portfolio), a heavy skew towards more contemporary models might not be a bad strategy to start with.

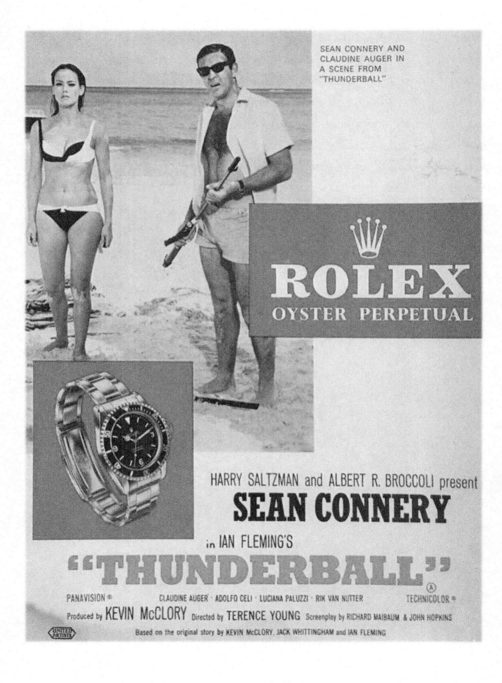

Limited Editions

Limited editions make in theory great investment candidates. The more limited the better. For truly limited-edition vintage watches, all the principles of vintage watch investing apply, with the caveat that they are simply even rarer than other models. By nature, when supply has ceased and production ended, every vintage watch is limited. But some naturally even more so than others! Also, limited, numbered editions of contemporary watches can yield good returns. Here things are again somewhat different as these watches usually attract grey market flippers that are looking for a quick buck via trading the watch after its release. Examples for such short-term returns from "hot" models are countless: most limited Omega Speedmaster re-editions have rapidly increased in value, also the new Omega Seamaster James Bond edition celebrating the 50th anniversary of the film *On Her Majesty's Secret Service* had a sudden value increase at first for the 7007 pieces produced. Often, however, a price drop follows such a *speculation bubble* in hot contemporary watches. Be aware that such newly released watches might be difficult to come by and require a close relationship with your AD. A very good relationship with your dealer is the only thing that helps, however, as said before, to get to such a relationship will often cost you a lot of money that you will most likely have to spend before on less investable watches. In turn, it is exactly this relationship that you risk by flipping the hot watch you received from him. The dealer has no control over his supply but can freely allocate his shipments. In 99 percent of cases, he will not be amazed if he discovers you flipped your watch (and yes, there are ways for him to find out). Such a quick flip strategy might hence work for certain people and can go well a couple of times, but short-term trading of contemporary watches is not what I recommend (except you really want to become a semi-professional grey market flipper, serving wholesale and retail clients in large volumes) and are not at all at the heart of this book.

Low Production Models

Low production watches refer not to a limited edition, but to particular models that watchmakers produce simply in low numbers, perhaps not even a proper series. The legendary Audemars Piguet Ref. 5402 A-Series limited to 1,000 pieces is an example, even if it was followed by additional productions runs later. Contemporary examples are also the already mentioned Tudor Harrods edition (only attainable in the famous Knightsbridge department store) or to a lesser extent the Tudor Pelagos LHD. The principle of supply and demand comes in here. However, these watches mainly become interesting once production has stopped and demand is starting to develop slowly. Low production models are certainly a trickier field of watch investing, but I nevertheless want to mention it. Since the demand for these watches is much more dependent on a limited number of potential collectors (and some investors), prices might act far more volatile, and it boils down to how much a limited set of buyers is willing to pay.

Impact of Contemporary Production

An important particularity of the vintage watch market is that it can often track the fortunes of modern watches surprisingly closely. The list of anecdotic evidence is exhaustive. For example, interest in historical Patek Philippe Nautilus references spiked massively when the watch celebrated its 40th anniversary in autumn 2016. Similarly, prices of vintage Rolex Daytonas increased only really after their contemporary counterparts (in particular the Ref. 116520) was an increasingly hard-to-get watch at ADs for decades. Another example is the rise of vintage Tudor watch prices in the last couple of years, coinciding with the brand's sensational return to form. Hitherto many Tudor pieces are now commanding significantly higher sale prices than a decade ago. The Big Block chronographs and French Navy MilSubs are already out of sight for many investors but interest spreads still to the more attainable models, and it's a fair bet that almost any vintage sports watch from Tudor still has appreciation left in it.

Iconic Watches

No matter whether a watch is contemporary or vintage, iconic watches with cult status will always form a sound base in any investment portfolio as these watches are not only the ones most likely to retain their value but also have a great perspective to increase even further in value–at least in line with the manufacturer's retail price increases. Well researched, it is hard to gain an edge when trying to buy an icon, but they offer in turn a great basis for any portfolio with the potential for steady, dependable gains and very limited downside. Next to the most coveted Rolex sports models (Daytona, Submariner, GMT, and Sea-dweller), Patek Philippe Nautilus models are examples of iconic, highly investable timepieces. It does matter less if we focus on the *original* Nautilus Ref. 3700 or the modern interpretation of it in the form of the 5711. These iconic timepieces will be unlikely found as a bargain at any dealer, and the new, contemporary versions often have year-long waiting lists, facts that make them even better investment pieces. Another favorite pick in the icon category is a different design by watchmaking mastermind Gerald Genta, the Audemars Piguet Royal Oak. Depending on the budget you can focus on contemporary references such as Ref. 15202 or earlier ones such as Ref. 15300 or Ref. 14790 (or of course, go all-in with the mighty Ref. 5402, the original Jumbo). Truly investable are especially the earlier models with the traditional Audemars Piguet font. There are many other examples of such iconic watches that are slowly creeping up in value but are at the same time highly liquid and easily sellable. You can hardly go wrong with putting some of these cult pieces in your portfolio as a strong foundation.

Liquidity

Closely related to the cult status of an iconic watch and breadth of demand for a watch is its liquidity, a term that describes how quickly one can re-sell a certain watch. For a watch investor, the liquidity of its pieces is an important component to consider as part of the portfolio construction process. It can make sense— depending on the individual circumstances— to hold a selection of very liquid watches (i.e. watches that are in very high demand and very quickly sellable with minimal or no loss). If you need to sell parts of your portfolio at a certain point, a forced sale (rather than waiting for a proper auction) might jeopardize your returns if all of your portfolio is made up of less liquid highly complicated pieces that are best being sold at auctions. Hence, it is advisable to keep a base layer of liquid pieces to adjust your portfolio quickly and with minimal transaction costs. The liquidity of your portfolio can be further improved by lowering the overall headline price of the timepieces you hold as the potential audience is naturally larger. Some watches with high liquidity are all references of the Paul Newman Rolex in the high value spectrum, steel Patek Philippe Nautilus variations in the mid-to-high spectrum as well as all steel Rolex GMTs, Sea-dwellers or Submariners in the (relatively) low-value spectrum. Remember that auction houses chose their lots one by one. This means they often on purpose seek to create bottlenecks for specific models in the market to boost demand for a certain type of watches. While this might have a positive effect on the auction price (and commissions for the auctioneer), it might become tricky and a project of several months, or even years, to sell an ensemble of higher-priced complicated timepieces. If you need the liquidity exactly then, you might get a problem.

Blue Chip Brands

The following section gives a very brief overview of the history of some of the key investment-grade brands, the *blue chips* of watchmaking so to say. This knowledge shall just give you the necessary bare-minimum background to ultimately better understand overall pricing and investment dynamics. It is obviously no replacement for your deep dive research via specialist book bands, auction catalogs, forums and social media (note: *investment models* in this chapter denotes simply investment-grade watches I find attractive at the time of publication).

Rolex

Heritage:	★★★★★
Quality:	★★★★★
Craftsmanship:	★★★★☆
Limited editions:	rare
Vintage market:	very developed

Traits: tool watch of choice (pilots, divers), engineering & ruggedness
Investment models: Zenith Daytonas, early Explorers, MilSubs

Overview:
Co-founded originally in London by German-born Hans Wilsdorf, the company famous for the crown has been headquartered in Geneva, Switzerland since 1919. Like few other brands, the success of the wristwatch today can be attributed to Rolex and its countless technical innovations. Today, Rolex is the most well-known luxury watch manufacturer. In a quest to produce simple but extremely effective and durable watches Rolex focused less on finishing and ornamenting complicated pieces than its Swiss neighbors. Rolex's professional watches are robust, purpose-built timepieces designed to withstand even the most

rigorous use. Its pre-WWII innovations include the famous water-resistant and dustproof *Oyster* case and the self-winding *Perpetual* technology. These would later also form the basis for many of their sports watches, such as the Submariner, Sea-dweller and GMT-Master.

Launched in 1963, the Cosmograph Daytona can today be considered the godfather of vintage watches and it's amongst the most iconic and coveted of all investment-grade watches. Other highly sought-after investment-grade models include their most complicated vintage watches with complications—a rarity for Rolex—such as the triple calendar chronograph or moon phase models. Of course there is the Submariner, the watch of choice of the early James Bond. Here especially early "big-crown" models and military-issued variants are of highest investment-grade. Not every Rolex is investable, and collectors and investors tend to gravitate primarily towards the brand's professional line that generally receives most attention and the highest auction bids. Datejust, Air-King or the pre-2020 Oyster Perpetual might keep a steady resale value but are unlikely to appreciate a lot or outperform inflation.

Audemars Piguet

Heritage:	★★★★★
Quality:	★★★★★
Craftsmanship:	★★★★★
Limited editions:	very rare
Vintage market:	developed

Traits: holy trinity, home of Genta's sports icon, Gianni Agnelli's choice
Investment models: early & mid-sized Royal Oaks, early Offshores

Overview:

The holy trinity member and specialist for finishing and technical complications was established in 1881 in Le Brassus, Switzerland. Audemars Piguet never ceases to impress with a rich history of creating bold, even audacious, timepieces underpinned by traditional watchmaking skills. Together with Patek Philippe, the brand is one of only two major manufacturers still owned by the founding family. Since its earliest days, "AP" has been considered a leader in the field of minute repeaters and grande complication watches and stands for high horology at its finest. The company is devoted to preserving the history of watchmaking in the Vallée de Joux, showcased at their newly opened superb museum in Le Brassus. Nowadays, it is best known for its Royal Oak models, the revolutionary luxury sports watch launched in 1972 by superstar designer Gerald Genta. Classic Royal Oaks of all ages are highly investable and see record-breaking demand as they not only represent a revolution in watch design and technical finesse but also incorporate everything luxury sports watches are supposed to be. When first launched, the Royal Oak didn't make a huge splash; however, opinions have shifted over the course of the last five decades and made the model today one of the most important icons in the watch industry.

Other investment-grade models of the brand include early minute repeaters, vintage chronographs, and perpetual calendars as well as the beginnings of the Offshore line-up. Less investable are the Jules and Millenary lines. Similarly to Rolex and Patek Philippe, within the past few years we have seen public demand for the brand's steel watches far exceed annual production numbers.

Patek Philippe

Heritage:	★★★★★
Quality:	★★★★★
Craftsmanship:	★★★★★
Limited editions:	ultra-rare
Vintage market:	very developed

Traits: holy trinity, highest quality craftsmanship, king of the hill

Investment models: chronographs (Refs. 130, 530), early Aquanauts

Overview:

Patek Philippe is no less than the prime example of a superlative watch manufacturer. Since its founding in 1839, the Geneva-based manufacturer and holy trinity member stands for horology at the highest level. Patek Philippe is often seen as king of the hill and has kept surprising with superbly crafted timepieces fitted with some of watchmaking's most prestigious complications. Over almost 200 years and via dozens of calibers, mechanical complication masterpieces and 100+ patents, Patek Philippe has evolved into the ultimate investment brand making them nearly crisis-proof additions to any investment portfolio. Today, Patek is known for producing not only some of the most important timepieces in history but also some of the most complicated. Traditional and conservative designs alike can be found across the decades-reaching line-up of the house. Well-known for the world's most complicated watch for half a century the family-owned company still holds the highest number of world records for results at any auction. For collectors and investors alike, key models in the watch hierarchy include the Ref. 1518, the world's first serially produced perpetual calendar chronograph, and its successor, the Ref. 2499. Other high-investment-grade models include perpetual calendars such as the Ref. 1526, 3448 and 3450 as well as several sought-after split-seconds chronographs. Patek is also famously known for the iconic Gerald Genta-designed Nautilus, first introduced in 1976 as the Ref. 3700.

Over the years, Patek invested heavily in marketing campaigns that focus on its watches as heirlooms. They recognized earlier than other brands that watches are not only timekeepers but also investment-grade items. Also the founding family started to buy back important watches for their museum to preserve and explain heritage. However the Patek brand does not always translate immediately into value appreciation. In fact, some of the company's signature timepieces such as the simple Calatrava dress watches, still struggle to keep their value.

Omega

Heritage:	★★★★☆
Quality:	★★★☆☆
Craftsmanship:	★★★☆☆
Limited Editions:	rare
Vintage market:	growing

Traits: chronometer accuracy, first watch on the moon
Investment models: rare Speedmasters (Ed White, Tin Tin)

Overview:

This firm's history dates back to 1848, when Louis Brandt founded it in La Chaux de Fonds. In 1903, it changed its name to Omega, becoming the only watch brand in history to have been named after one of its own movements. As a manufacturer of accurate, yet affordable watches, its stellar reputation gave Omega in 1932 the honor of timing the Olympic Games. Three decades later, its Speedmaster was chosen by NASA to become the first wristwatch to be worn on the moon. Known for their Master Chronometer Certificate, Omegas have been seen on the wrists of presidents, kings, astronauts, and fictional spies, making many of its watches highly sought-after on the pre-owned market and a sound addition to any investment portfolio. Key models coveted by collectors include their first oversized water-resistant chronograph (Ref. 2077), early Speedmaster models (e.g. CK 2915, 2998), military-issued versions of the Seamaster and oversized chronometer models such as those fitted with their caliber 30T2Rg. Until recently they were not known for blow-out results at auctions, most of the vintage market was focused on Speedmasters, Seamasters or (Genta-designed) Constellations. Given the comparatively low entry prices and high production volumes, the market can at times be difficult to maneuver and brings surprises.

F.P. Journe

Heritage:	★★☆☆☆
Quality:	★★★★★
Craftsmanship:	★★★★★
Limited Editions:	ultra-rare
Vintage market:	n/a

Traits: independence, innovation, creativity, low production
Investment models: Vagabondage series, Elegante 48

Overview:

Founded only in 1999 by François-Paul Journe, the brand is still young but already regarded by some of world's savviest collectors and investors as a distinguished manufacturer with centuries of heritage. As an independent watchmaker, Journe makes watches irrespective of trends and tends to break rules. Journe picked up the L'Aiguille d'Or already twice. Key investment-grade models include the Résonance, tourbillon wristwatches, the limited-edition Vagabondage series as well as the innovative, yet highly controversial Elegante 48. Most sought-after are his earliest *souscription* watches, released in the first year of operation. By virtue of their highly limited production numbers, Journe timepieces tend to do very well at auctions and don't show up a lot at dealers. In 2017, its Monopusher Split-Seconds Chronograph fetched CHF 1.2 million, unseating the Philippe Dufour Duality as the most expensive independent watchmaker's timepiece sold at an auction. The degree of positive price momentum from both investors as well as collectors, coupled with Journe's state-of-the-art watchmaking skill and ultra-low-production numbers for unique models, gives many high-quality pieces of the brand excellent prospects for future value appreciation.

Part III – Chapter Summary:

- Like most assets, also the value of a watch on the secondary market is driven by the basic law of supply and demand
- There are three overlapping areas that are critical for any watch and form the value triangle: we call them *Core*, *Mechanical*, and *Intrinsic* Value
- Immaculate dials, perfectly maintained movements and cases in pristine condition make up the Core Value. Relative rarity of a model as well as other softer factors drive the Intrinsic Value. Horological complications are most important for the Mechanical Value of a watch
- Investability of a watch brand follows a pyramid structure with Patek and Rolex occupying the top of it (closely followed by Audemars Piguet)

Part IV: How To Invest In Watches

The Investment Process

"I never regret a watch I bought. Many times, I have regretted the watches I haven't bought."

> – Alfredo Paramico, Supercollector-Investor
> (Private Air, 2015)

The process of buying a classic watch can generally be divided into two phases: the pre-acquisition phase, which consists of *knowledge building, screening, due diligence* and *valuation*, as well as the post-acquisition phase, which consists of *storage* and *exit*. In this part of the book I will walk you through each of these steps and point towards their respective pitfalls and specialties.

Pre-Acquisition Phase

Knowledge Building

We have mentioned throughout this book that the first crucial step for any watch novice is to know watches, i.e. build brand and model specific knowledge. Importantly, this step needs to happen *ahead* of narrowing down on a specific piece that you intend to purchase. For example, let's assume you would like to add an icon watch to your portfolio and stumble upon an interesting Audemars Piguet Royal Oak Jumbo Ref. 5204 at a local shop or on the Instagram page of a renowned online dealer. So far, you have been following the brand from a high-level perspective. And while the price seems fair at first glance for the offered condition, you are neither an expert in Royal Oaks nor the Jumbo model in particular. The last thing you want to do now is dive directly into the purchase process, forgoing the *due diligence* phase. In fact, at this first educational stage you shouldn't spend the majority of your time browsing, i.e. looking for actual models in the market (something watch investment novices tend to focus first the majority of their time), but instead focus on building knowledge about the brand and reference in question.

Only after you have built the required knowledge you can start the actual hunt. I know the temptation to constantly screen for bargains is hard to resist at times, but if you intend to purchase a watch as an investment it cannot be emphasized enough that research needs to come first. Information gathering way ahead of a purchase is the secret ingredient that all successful watch investors share in their recipe. Obviously, this requires a high degree of patience, interest and passion. Focusing on the dopamine kick that arises from the feeling of ownership is not enough if you want to continuously acquire models that will appreciate in value. If you cannot help but fall asleep when observing the fine differences in dials or studying the evolution of a particular reference, then you will not be able to stick to the required investment process successfully over the long run. Obviously, you will do *some* browsing also during this stage. But as a committed watch investor, you have to do the work first: gather essential information, read virtually everything relevant to a specific reference you can find, stay focused and don't let your emotions overwhelm you. Therefore I usually advise novices to focus on one brand and within that brand one model first.

Only gradually should you start extending your knowledge across references and brands. From analyzing hundreds of watches and most major classic watch brands I have learned never to spread knowledge too thinly. I repeat myself here, but if there is only one takeaway from this book it would be never to compromise on the initial research you do. Only a meticulous approach will help you to gain an edge over the vast majority of collectors, who can work with a much broader, superficial approach and buy whatever they like and what comes to the market irrespective of longer-term value developments. Striving for deep knowledge that is hard to replace will give you that small but crucial informational advantage over the average watch buyer.

Screening

After building sufficient knowledge about a particular reference for a good amount of time, you will inevitably transition into the *Screening* period and start browsing more and more. Most watch investors, including myself, tend to love this phase the most. It is this phase that gives you that special kick once you stumble upon an interesting timepiece for sale on Instagram or you receive that email from your favorite dealer. In this phase you look out for particular references that you previously researched and that lie within your investment criteria and budget. You will find yourself developing your personal list of go-to dealers online as well as offline; you will start attending auctions, vintage watch fairs and gatherings and hopefully make new friends while discussing your future purchases with fellow watch investors and collectors.

There are many ways to conduct screening and everybody develops his own process over time. When I look at my personal screening process today, it is very clear that, although it became inevitably more digital, my heart still lies in browsing offline. In particular I still adore visiting dealers face-to-face. True, most dealers have online presences and there are many trusted online sources to buy from. However, nothing replaces a face-to-face conversation and the intellectual satisfaction I get from it. Still, some of the best investment purchases I made were not from dealers but bought directly from other collectors (ideally when they were trying to free up funds for a new project) or fellow investors seeking to realize previous gains. Over the last few years the ascent of online deals has shaken up the traditional purchase dynamics somewhat, especially for the neo-vintage market. Technology has also made its way into the watch market and—at least in terms of volumes—the majority of watches will soon be sold via digital platforms and online auctions.

In-person deals were the way to go before online buying arose. While some people call it outdated, sometimes it is still the most feasible way to purchase a watch (for example if you happen to be in a safe city and want

143

a quick transaction). I personally conducted several deals in cities ranging from London to L.A. and never had any major issues. Ideally, in-person deals should be conducted always in secure public locations with no cash changing hands. In theory, the best option has always been to meet at the watch buyer's bank of choice. There you can easily conduct the wire transfer and handover (in front of a third person if you so wish) and you are more secured against a potential fraud scheme with cameras and security staff present. Public areas within luxury hotels are another fairly decent spot. In the end it is key to always remain skeptical, avoid deals and requests that are too good to be true and make your way around dubious cash-deals and sketchy buyers or sellers.

On the digital side things are evolving quickly. While platforms such as eBay or member-to-member sales corners in dedicated forums have already been around for ages, new marketplaces and dealer websites are emerging rapidly and even the social media platform Instagram has gained a strong position in the sub $10k segment. Importantly, with the ascent of marketplace websites like Chrono24 and the increasingly fierce battle of auction houses, the market for mid-to-high price range watches has become already more efficient than it used to be in the past. A friend of mine, eager to start investing in watches, asked me recently over a glass of wine how I buy my investment watches nowadays and where I think the journey will lead to. What I told him is that I use today a multitude of various channels and recommended him to be open to such a hybrid approach. It always depends on the budget and watch in question, but even on websites like eBay I have been able to acquire excellent Zenith or Longines models in the lower price range, and that was long before eBay started offering authenticated pieces.

Often somewhat disregarded as "the bay" it is still a decent marketplace to screen for watches and it constantly updates its service offering and security features specifically for luxury items. Other auction websites and platforms have appeared and disappeared over the last years, but eBay is still defending the crown among the generalist platforms. Then there are dedicated watch marketplaces, with Chrono24 being the leading platform by far. While things are evolving quickly, as of today, I would say that of all the platforms out there Chrono24 and eBay remain the largest and most regimented platforms for buying watches online (and doing so in a secure fashion). Their buyer protection is not perfect but robust, and the feedback system is a reliable grading scale for evaluating seller longevity and quality. Sellers with years of experience and hundreds of feedback ratings generally have worked for years to create their reputations and have a large incentive to preserve them. Sure, you can still fake ratings, but the chances are lower, and the risk is not systematic. Obviously, there is also Craigslist in the US, which I rarely ever used being based in Europe.

When purchasing a watch through Chrono24 or eBay, make always sure to actually purchase the watch through the site as it is the most secure way. Any attempt by a seller to advertise a watch on a site such as eBay while requesting an off-site transaction is not only against the policy but should raise a red flag. Countless instances of fraud have resulted from people agreeing to take a transaction from the actual online platform to a private party deal only to save a few bucks on fees. Don't be the next fool to go that route. When buying from an online marketplace, do look for high feedback ratings, and ensure that a watch dealer's rating is the cumulative product of its experience as a seller rather than a buyer. Once a seller accumulates years of feedback reputation and transaction history, a true financial theft scam is rather inconceivable. For a professional sellers it's much easier to conduct additional due diligence than for a private seller. Hence, I recommend novice investors to focus in the beginning on professional sellers when buying online.

Outside of the actual platform I like to pay attention to identifying other signs of a seller's reputation and want to see that he is actually investing in it. A professional website that is kept up to date and marks a big investment for the seller (or a solid Instagram account with a decent following and lots of real interaction) is what I am after. Ideally, I am looking for real customer references, not anonymous testimonials.

145

As mentioned before, auctions have gone a long way over the last decade or so from being low-key, small gatherings of a small inner-circle to a grand spectacle (especially if Aurel Bacs stands on the rostrum). With the ascent of online auctions and the increasing popularity of physical auctions, today you are spoiled for choice when considering whether to attend an auction (virtually) once you've screened and like the catalogue. Sure, nothing compares with the in-person experience and the interactions with like-minded people between the sales of the lots. However, aside from the traditional phone option, you can nowadays often also bid online in real-time; an option for maximum privacy and something that might be increasingly beneficial the higher the value of the acquired timepieces is.

Excursus: Auction Algebra

No matter if in-person or remotely, what you will be bidding is always the hammer price that goes to the consignor who supplied the watch to the auction house. On top of that you have to pay a commission fee to the auction house for their services. This fee differs according to the value and setup of the auction and can be seen in the respective auction invitation letter or on the website. Amongst others, the services of the auction house include the provision of an estimate price, where an expert gives an (more or less) independent value appraisal. Commission plus hammer price together make up the actual sale price. The auction starts with the so-called reserve price, the minimum price acceptable for the seller. Auction houses provide a total guarantee of the authenticity of a piece and inspect it in great detail. Hence, they are most certainly the safest way to screen for and acquire an authentic timepiece. That safety and privacy, however, comes at a price tag that you have to factor in during your screening.

Only once you've found a suitable timepiece at a reputable source that fits your investment goals you transition into the next phase, the due diligence.

146

Due Diligence

"Often, the best collector is not the one with the deepest pockets but the one with the best knowledge".

– Aurel Bacs (Hashtag Legend, 2016)

The *due diligence* can take place virtually or in-person and will typically involve you (*primary* due diligence) as well as potentially third parties and experts (*secondary* due diligence). Step one of every due diligence process will be the authenticity check where you determine the authenticity or genuineness of the watch in question. Due to the vast differences in the degree of authenticity a watch can have nowadays, I will give you a simple scoring scheme as decision support, which we will introduce in a minute. This rating shall help you to better compare and analyze target investments. In the beginning you may as well consider building a good relationship with an external expert or more advanced investor who can help you out with a second opinion, similarity to a PPI that you would conduct on a classic car. Especially in the major metropoles and for online timepieces this is easily feasible. Right after you have assessed and graded the authenticity, you will focus on the actual (technical) condition of the watch.

Technical evaluation and the authenticity check naturally overlap as they are done in one process and typically involve taking a look at the inside of the watch. As mentioned before, it is unlikely that with some basic know-how you will run into a Chinese replica movement after looking at the open case (although Asian replica producers even try to counterfeit for example Rolex in-house movements such as the caliber 4310 in their replicas and work with an increasing degree of sophistication). Especially the finish is typically a rather easy tell and with a loupe and open case-back fakes are still noticeable even by novices (and especially after you've completed your homework and built the essential knowledge).

The problem of *frankening* is in my view the much bigger issue. Over the years, vintage watches can change due to wear and tear as well as through repair and maintenance work. If the previous owner had chosen to replace certain parts with non-original or aftermarket parts, this might be already a frankening issue. The question of this highly controversial topic is what is really still authentic and where does forgery start? Nowadays, virtually every single vintage watch spare part can be publicly bought via forums, Instagram, eBay or in special Facebook groups. With enough money in your bank account also a genuine Paul Newman dial or a Double Red Sea-dweller dial is not a problem. And I am not talking just about dials; handsets, pearls, movements, you name it—every single part is available to buy. Obviously, parts for the most sought-after pieces can easily burn a deep hole in your pocket.

Also, the practice of restoring worn-down watches to bring them closer to an acceptable condition is becoming more and more omnipresent. And in theory there is also no problem with it, but the problem is one of disclosure. When you are paying for all-original condition, you have to get it. And that's where things start to get more difficult and you have to be deep in the details of the reference in question. For example, with a Rolex always look between the lugs and watch out for the serial number as it can give you an indication whether you are looking at a replacement case (a 44 at the beginning would indicate that for Rolexes). Fortunately there are amazing resources that point you to things like this. And failure to pay attention can be costly. The watch world is here (at least today) still different from the classic car community. A set of replaced dials damages the value of a watch significantly more than a new dashboard in Porsche 912E, even if genuine.

So where does a frankenwatch start? Clearly, changing the dial color for a Rolex is too much; also non-genuine parts are no question, but what about things like the glass or the crown? Does changing the glass from impractical, scratchy plexy to more contemporary and practical sapphire glass for a 30-year-old Rolex make it an uninvestable frankenwatch? What about a service dial or a new crown? A new or after-market bezel? To take the emotion and subjective aspect out of this discussion, I provide below a guide for the different classes of authenticity. We should count only the first three categories as investment-grade watches, i.e. watches that you should be buying for investment purposes. Depending on the type of watch, wear and tear and resulting repairs play a different role in the valuation. While for an **IWC Beobachtungsuhr**—a 70-plus-year-old military watch that has spent at least some of its lifetime under harsh conditions in the field—it is not big a problem if the watch has even significant signs of wear. As you might imagine, the story is very different for a rose-gold perpetual calendar dress watch such as the Patek Philippe Ref. 3970. Sure, the military watch would enter a category lower if, for example, the pushers had been replaced with a non-original part at some point in the past. But a certain degree of scratches, dents or other signs of wear would not influence its value that much or make it uninvestable. Again, specific knowledge about the reference in question is key here.

Investing in Watches – Authenticity Rating

Category AAA (100%)

- Watch in completely original factory condition
- Only technical maintenance and repairs with original parts by authorized watch experts

Category AA (90%)

- Only technical maintenance and minor repairs with non-visible original parts by authorized watch experts

Category A (80%)

- Minor optical refurbishment of selected visible parts (dial, case) to bring the watch closer back to factory condition

Category B-C (40-70%)

- More than minor optical refurbishment of selected parts (dial, case) to bring the watch closer back to factory condition

Category D (<40%)

- Parts or components have been replaced with non-genuine parts ("Frankenwatch") / parts from other watches ("marriage watch")
- Watch only partially original

Category E (0%)

- Replica base with genuine parts, e.g. dial, case, etc. ("Superfranken")

To analyze the authenticity of a watch according to this checklist, beginners should either consult an expert or prepare themselves extensively for the check of a certain model.

Due Diligence & Study Resources

You are in a privileged position today. The internet has become the single most important and useful resource when analyzing watches. There are fantastic websites for virtually all brands and the landscape is evolving too quickly to capture it completely in this book. And then there is the fantastic literature from the likes of Mondani and Goldberger. Some of my favorite and most enduring and precious resources are listed here below. Many of these books are notoriously hard to get, and you will have to check dealers, Amazon second-hand offerings, eBay & Co. regularly to catch one of these. Prices tend to be on the high side, but resale value is equally high.

Here's a mix of free and paid due diligence resources I absolutely recommend:

- **Rolex Passion Report** *(Website), Philipp Stahl, Free*
  Rolex Passion Report is a website where Philipp Stahl and friends share their passion for vintage Rolex & Tudor watches. A must-have in your browser favourites.

- **Collectability** *(Website), John Reardon, Free*
  Released in late 2019 by John Reardon, former head of watches at Christie's, Collectability has immediately become the ultimate vintage Patek Philippe resource.

- **100 Superlative Rolex Watches** *(Amazon), Goldberger*
  A must-have bible for every Rolex investor. Supercollector Auro Montanari, aka John Goldberger introduces here 100 Rolex models (there is an iPad/iPhone app which is great for hunting out in the field).

- **Patek Philippe: Cult Object and Investment** *(Amazon), Mehltretter*
  With detailed descriptions and photos, Mehltretter highlights Patek Philippe watches as crisis-proof additions to an investment portfolio.

- **Daytona Perpetual,** *(Website), Papaleo*
  After his mind-blowing Ultimate Rolex Daytona publication, Pucci Papaleo, one of the most influential man in the world of vintage Daytonas, here shares his wealth of knowledge about Perpetual Daytonas. Sits right on my sofa table!

Below is a list of some more excellent printed resources that you should absolutely add to your repertoire if you get a hand on them:

- **Watches By Hodinkee** (Website)
- **Royal Oak** (Amazon)
- **Collecting Nautilus & Modern Patek Philippe** (Amazon), Mondani / Patrizzi
- **Audemars Piguet: Master Watchmaker Since 1875**
- **Patrizzi Pocket Expert Series**, (Amazon), Patrizzi
- **Pocket Expert: The Magical White Cartier Bianco**
- **Patek Philippe Steel Watches**, (Website), Goldberger
- **Patek Philippe Museum Catalog**: Montres Patek Philippe, Vol. 1 & 2
- **Rolex Daytona** (Amazon), Mondani / Patrizzi
- **Vintage Panerai: The References, 1950s-1960s**
- **Heuer Carrera Chronographs 1963-1985**
- **Patek Philippe – Timepieces for Royalty 1850-1910**, 2005
- **Collecting Patek Philippe Wristwatches**, Vol. 1, 2, & 3, 2005, Patrizzi
- **Reference Guides for the Nautilus 3700 and Amagnetic 3417**, 2017-19, Mstanga
- **Patek Philippe in America Men's Reference Guide**, 2010, Reardon
- **Uhren von Patek Philippe**, Limited Edition, 1980, Vogel

Aside from these printed resources above, also (online) catalogues of the big auction houses are incredibly useful. My favorites include:

- **Game Changers,** New York Auction, 2019, Phillips
- **The Geneva Watch Auction,** Edition One – Eight, Phillips
- **Important Watch Auction Catalogues,** Christie's
- **Patek Philippe 175ᵗʰ Anniversary Theme Auction,** 2014, Christie's
- **The Art of Patek Philippe,** 150ᵗʰ Anniversary, Vol. 1 & 2, 1989, Antiquorum
- **The Art of Patek Philippe,** 1999, Antiquorum

Frankly, there are countless more auction catalogues and several book bands in my library that could have been added to this list. I cannot emphasize enough the importance of building an extensive library of physical and digital auction catalogs. Another rather new due diligence option is social media. Over the last few years especially Instagram has developed into an exceptional watch community.

Not only can you use this community to identify experts for certain models, but watch experts and collectors are usually very helpful and like to share their knowledge. By searching with hashtags such as #royaloak5204 or #rolex1680 you have easy access to dealers, watch owners and experts. Some people prefer to count on other sources, but I have found Instagram is developing into one of the most useful modern resources to analyze and study timepieces.

Excursus: Red Flags & Watch Scams

Jumping on the (vintage) watch train can clearly yield an investor stellar returns. But if not done with vigilance and care, there may be a perfect storm waiting for investors over the horizon. The emergence of replicas and frankenwatches can make watch investing a dangerous sea to sail on for the unprepared. As mentioned, also the watch world is not immune to replicas and fakes. Replicas are an unfortunate trend and since demand will likely stay strong, this is always a problem watch investors simply have to cope with. Manufacturers will never be able to do something against the fake watch industry as long as there are enough people who—for whatever reason—want to buy fake watches. In this chapter we give you a brief overview of the dangerous world of replicas and frankenwatches and how to effectively maneuver around the threats posed by them.

Sadly, the global market for replica watches is booming like never before. The replication quality and attention to details of Chinese replicas has sadly increased massively over the last decade. We are not referring to cheap knock-off Rolexes that are sold on the beaches of Rimini or Ibiza by flying merchants. With better manufacturing conditions as part of the ongoing industrialization in China, the quality of so-called replicas, or "reps" for short, has recently gone through the roof. The replicas today are carefully re-engineered pieces by factories that operate under names such as Noob, ARF or BP and that use the original watch as a model for their plagiarism. On top of that, there's an active community of several tens of thousands of replica watch enthusiasts who continuously point replica manufacturers to the flaws of each new batch released. Every replica will start with a version 1 and then is followed by a version 2, which then might have for example a better copied date wheel and better dimensions, and so on until a say version 7 arrives, which has been through several iterations with virtually everything that is low hanging fruit—for the untrained eye—flawlessly replicated. This watch would then be called a "super rep". These watches retail for $400–$800, sometimes even more, an insane price for a fake watch. While this might not bother the watch enthusiast who wants to buy only brand-new watches from authorized dealers, this becomes a growing problem for the secondhand watch market. Yes, you will be able to spot obvious flaws such as a replica movement after a few hours of studying watches, but the problem is not as simple as that.

First of all, people have started mixing the significantly cheaper replica parts with original pieces. An example would be to use a replica dial or crown for a vintage Rolex Submariner Ref. 1680. We call this then a "franken" watch, i.e. a watch that is no longer 100 percent original and resembles Frankenstein's Monster. Most recently, even in-house movements are being replicated; while the manufacturing precision and quality control differs greatly, the untrained eye will have more difficulties than before when cheap Chinese movements were used.

Secondly, there are watch builds where the primary donor is a replica watch and it is just frankened with the most obvious original parts such as the dial. This becomes a huge problem as the dial is the central focus point for most collectors and an original dial might give a potential examiner some undeserved relief and then reduce his attentiveness regarding other flaws.

Third, there's a growing group of replica watch enthusiasts called mooders. These are often former independent watch smiths that were attracted by the challenge (or money involved) of frankening watches and specialize in this work. Some of them explicitly specialize in techniques to give a replica vintage watch, such as a Rolex GMT, that comes fresh out of the Chinese factory the best possible 25-year-old look by recreating tropical dials, re-luming, etc. The results are often scarily astonishing. Other mooders are specialized in constructing superfrankens of contemporary and vintage pieces that are sold in online forums for up to $4k. Such a superfranken might even feature a majority of genuine parts such as dial, crown, bezel and crystal, sometimes even movement. What a crazy world! I was invited back in 2019 to a viewing of several of these replica pieces and I can say *that—without a 10x loupe, the Goldberger App or a genuine example next to it—only a very small percentage of the watch world would have been able to tell the difference between a real Rolex Submariner and a $600 replica. This percentage gets even smaller when we are talking about mooded vintage replica Rolexes, where sometimes even the caliber has been customized and you are less accustomed to the model. Only equipped with original auction catalogs and the special literature that contains high-quality pictures of the original caliber do you stand a chance against these frankenwatches; this is why it is crucial to equip yourself with the right due diligence resources.*

If you want so, the good part is that, as of today, the fake market focuses primarily on contemporary watches and the vintage and neo-vintage products are of poor quality and, in most cases, more easily spotted. It gets much more difficult when some independent watch smith invested $4,000 to replicate a Daytona Ref. 6263, but at least here the movement still tells the truth, even without any loupe. This is different for a contemporary Daytona Ref. 116500LN, where today even the movement looks at first glance like all-Rolex. Last but not least, I need to mention that the term franken is not only used for replica parts and genuine parts in combination. Even parts of a wrong reference in theory would create a Franken watch. This problem, for example, is common for one of the most iconic and sought-after entry-level watches, the Omega Speedmaster Professional, the Moonwatch. Over the years (esp. between 1960–1980), Omega released so many different sub-references that watch smiths and collectors started to use parts of the different references interchangeably; "It is still a Speedmaster so why not swap the case back when one can save a couple of bucks?" was the thinking in the past. Well, the watch community today certainly doesn't think so and this has created a disease that many of the Speedmasters in the vintage world suffer from.

Fake Busters: Spotting A Super-Rep

Rolex Submariner Ref. 116610LN

Case: difficult tell – nowadays often made with 904L steel (like top-grade metal used in the real watch). Brushing is less fine on cheaper replicas, but superreps came a long way

Bezel: easy tell - clicking and feeling are immediate giveaways if you handled genuine model before

Pearl: difficult tell – most replicas are very close to the gen at shape, color and jade-like effect; hole on the ceramic insert does now take a gen pearl

Crystal: difficult tell – assembly usually no giveaway and clean. Date font can be a give-away even without loupe, but you might need a genuine datewheel to compare

Hands: easy tell – under magnification edges are sharper and less carefully finished (no "3D effect")

Insert markers: easy tell – replicas using real platinum plated on the insert markers, but adhesive force of platinum makes it hard for forgers to shape details after plating. Under magnification fake inserts are dirty/darker. Cheaper replicas will even have whiter (non-platinum) inserts

Hacking seconds: easy tell for cheap reps – when pulling crown out all the way, second hand should stop moving ("hacking seconds"); fakes >$300 might use better mechanical movement and get the same result

Movement: easy tell – unscrewing the case back reveals most poor imitations (mostly used are ETA/Chinese copy movements with some masquerade modifications); Newest high-value replicas >$600 also replicate movement look, engravings and layout, but under magnification it's still a no-brainer to tell

Dial Font: not an easy tell – still, printing of font is usually off and not 100 percent perfect. Under magnification significantly less sharp (vs. super-crisp for genuine watch)

Clasp: easy tell – genuine clasp is beautifully finished inside and out with tight tolerances. Feels and sounds solid when folding and closing with easy link extension snapping tightly. Nicely finished coronet. Fake feels usually much cheaper and harder to handle

Valuation

– Juan-Carlos Torres, former CEO of Vacheron Constantin
(Lane, 2017)

Determining Fair Value

Hand in hand with the due diligence phase goes the determination of the fair value of a watch and the appropriate price you should pay for it as an investment. We discussed the most important drivers that determine the value of a watch such as its brand, condition, or provenance. For this we introduced three categories that help to deconstruct the valuation framework for a watch: Mechanical Value, Intrinsic Value and Core Value give you a better idea of the longer-term fair value of a watch rather than its current price alone.

Remember there is often a difference between the price and the value of any asset, even if in the first place you can only see its price. Pricing dynamics are much more short-term oriented and very much driven by trends, sentiment and fads. Price is of utmost relevance for watch flippers of contemporary watches; value is more important for the long-term investor. Like all investments, watches have a price determined by the market where the asset is traded. For any watch investment, the fair value must be higher than the purchase price to allow excess returns just above appreciation in line with inflation and manufacturer price increases.

In other words, you cannot buy a watch as a long-term investment if you are paying a price that truly equals its fair value. This would equal value storage but does not imply appreciation. Even for a contemporary *growth* model you must have some expectation of where the value will go in future; otherwise you will be at best compensated for inflation. It is crucial to also include potential maintenance costs or even repairs that have to be conducted, especially in the less pristine segment where not everything is mint and valued at several thousands of dollars. For example, if the balance shaft in a vintage piece is damaged and the manufacturer recently ran out of stock, the made-to-order replacement part can easily destroy the whole investment case before it even starts. A low-priced watch would then potentially suffer its economical death. Even if replacement parts are not out of stock and simply hard to get, an unplanned maintenance process can easily become time and money eroding.

In general we decide between *pricing* a model and determining its value *appreciation* potential. When it comes to pricing a watch, we are mostly speaking about comparable watch transactions, where very similar (ideally almost identical) watches of the same reference have been sold recently. Auction prices can be tracked, plotted and aggregated and can give initial guidance when determining the right price. Online watch communities are very helpful here as well. Then there are printed catalogs that appear every year that can also serve as a quick reference point. Rather than using only one source, a multi-faceted approach that combines various sources is typically best when pricing a model. This method of pricing is certainly looking in the rear-view mirror but has proven to be a decent measure of price determination. At the end of the day, watches are not complex corporations, so the pricing process is more straightforward than for a listed company in the stock market.

Current list prices at online platforms and portals are a tricky thing. Prices on dealer websites and marketplaces like Chrono24 can be helpful but be careful that you take into account completed transactions rather than just listings. It is not uncommon for sellers to list certain models at very ambitious prices, so this data cannot always be taken seriously. Sometimes they are close to the fair value; sometimes they are fantasy or wildcard prices where sellers simply want to test the market in hopes of a (crazy) bid. Especially for rare models, it is crucial to have a profound understanding of the recent comparable transactions that have taken place in the public auction space. What you can see is that the more liquid a watch is the more accurately the listed price online reflects the actual value of the watch. This means that if you are looking at a Rolex Submariner Ref. 16610, the listed priced will track the watches value on average much closer than for a rare vintage reference that only appears once on the platform such as a COMEX Submariner.

After having analyzed the appropriate pricing of a watch, the next step is building your own view of its *value appreciation potential.* This step is certainly more art than science and builds on everything we said about the value drivers of a watch so far. As you saw in the checklist and sample analysis of the Audemars Piguet Ref. 14790ST in Part III, there is a range of factors involved in the valuation process and much of the work involved is a combination of knowledge, experience, an ear at the market and instinct. In a few minutes we will try to illustrate this even better by looking at another watch, a vintage Patek Ref. 3970. The process is never 100 percent repeatable for every model, but the key pillars remain the same no matter which watch is analyzed. Over time it will become more and more natural and you will become much quicker and more comfortable when determining the value potential of a future investment. However, you will be wrong at times and need to take the failure of your investment thesis into account when placing your bets. Obviously, you won't put all your eggs into one basket, but still you should always have a good idea not only of your upside potential but also how much you could lose if your thesis does not turn out as planned.

The risk-reward profile of your investment is best determined by having a look into the past. The potential for a loss in a particular investment can be judged best by studying previous price differences and auction results. If the watch has had a steady upward trend shown over the past years it is less likely that a sudden shortfall in demand will occur than when there were lots of ups and downs in the price tendency of a watch and the overall development is highly volatile.

Investment Horizon

If you arrive at a firm view that the watch you intend to acquire is undervalued/mispriced, the next step is to determine the time horizon of your potential investment. The investment horizon for a watch is the total length of time that the watch investor expects to hold the watch as part of his portfolio. This period is used to determine the investor's liquidity needs and desired portfolio risk exposure, which is in turn used to aid selection of a particular (set of) watch model(s). With some exceptions and exclusions (such as flipping of contemporary watches), a typical watch investment for me has a mid-to-long-term time horizon of more than five years. In some rather rare cases, a quick flip of a limited edition might be feasible, but, as mentioned before, this is not in focus here.

As a bare minimum, watch investors should be looking for returns that outperform the risk-free interest rate, i.e. long-term returns on safe government bonds, by a certain margin. Depending on the prevailing interest rate and inflation environment, the lack of interest or income of any sort and sole reliance on capital gains makes watches typically an even more attractive investment instrument in a low-interest-rate environment. However, despite the current risk-free interest rate being still near historical lows in the US and Europe, most watch investors I know still look for gross return for a blue-chip watch portfolio of at least five percent per year, always depending on their risk appetite.

Liquidity Profile

As mentioned before, the liquidity of a watch is an important investment criterion. Certain watches are highly liquid, while there are some pieces that offer nice return perspectives but are less easy to market and sell successfully. When acquiring a new piece or putting together a portfolio of timepieces, the watch investor has to bear in mind the liquidity profile and how it affects his overall portfolio. Models such as the Patek Philippe Nautilus or Rolex Daytona, are—especially in complete package and pristine condition—sellable within hours at a tight spread and at low costs.

Of course the liquidity of a watch might change over time and some years ago was not a given for models that are today virtually same-day sales. Such highly liquid watches can make up a stable core component of your watch portfolio, even if your assessment determines that no spectacular returns are likely. In contrast, more specialized niche timepieces such as a rare minute repeater higher-priced limited-edition models or models with unique provenance often tend to need a certain marketing period, e.g. in the form of an auction catalog, in order show their full value potential. However, bear in mind that lower liquidity also stands for a higher potential for outsized returns. For such pieces you have to look for the right sweet spot of demand in order to sell the watch successfully. Here it is not only crucial at which point of time but also in which geographical market you are selling the watch.

As you can see, there is no standard recipe when it comes to valuing and pricing watches. The former in particular is clearly an art, not a science. How to become better? By practice, experience and hard work. There is no magic formula and luck plays a certain role, especially when looking at a shorter time period and only a handful of watches. However, keep in mind that over the long-run it is your process and your due diligence that will determine the success of your overall portfolio as luck and randomness will equal out. If you limit your downside then retail price appreciation of current models and inflation will likely more than protect your investment and outperform interest rates on savings accounts already by a wide margin. And these are then only the models where you basically were wrong with your valuation assessment and where the market did not change its opinion about the piece you deemed undervalued. In short, heads you win; tails you don't lose. This is how watch investing should be done.

"Today, a collector needs to be chameleon. You can't afford to put all your eggs on one basket anymore. Ten years ago [...] I would have told you to keep and enjoy your pieces. Today, I think collectors need to be more pragmatic. When the value of your collection goes with the taste of the

market, it's important to be flexible and know when to enter and exit different things. I don't like this aspect very much, it feels like the stock market at times, but unfortunately, we are not in the same age where you collect what you like, and the value of your collection trickles up in value."

– Helmut Crott (A Collected Man, 2020)

Practice Makes the Master

As watches will never really be able to shake off uniqueness as one of their defining characteristics, automated uniform valuations will always remain a dream scenario. At least for the foreseeable future auction houses and online platforms will continue to serve as a reliable anchor for valuations and price determination. One way I learned to improve my valuation technique was to pick certain pieces in the catalog of an upcoming auction and then try to assess and replicate the (covered) auction house estimate by building my very own value range. After the auction I would then look at the results and try to understand in detail what happened. Sometimes the results were rather random and my estimates disappointing. But if you do this over and over you start to recognize patterns for certain models and get a better grasp of your very own personal biases (I for example had a natural tendency to discount dress watches too heavily and overvalue timepieces from houses such as IWC or Breguet). You can even do this retrospectively with an auction catalog and the actual results. I started to work through several catalogs like this before I seriously started to invest in higher-priced vintage pieces. Paying close attention to the most important international auction dynamics of houses such as Phillips, Christie's or Sotheby's is key and one of the most effective ways to improve your understanding of price and value dynamics.

Theft Schemes and Rip-Offs

As crucial as it is for a stock market investor to avoid pink-sheet frauds and pump-and-dump schemes, it's equally important for a watch investor to protect his portfolio from deception, fraud and theft. As with all markets where significant sums of money are on the table, the watch market also draws the attention of unfair players to it. In the liberal, unregulated, high-

163

stakes game of watch investing, there will always be some players who don't play right. In most cases, a deal does not scream shady business right away. Hence, you have to protect yourself in order to avoid fraud. In principle, watch investors encounter two key risks—misrepresentation and theft. While identity or financial theft schemes often draw financial predators from outside the watch space, a misrepresented product is typically much more common and generally involves a watch dealer or private seller. For this reason, it is not enough to simply confirm during your due diligence that the seller is a real person or documented past seller of luxury watches.

Attempted thefts can be thwarted by diligent attention to payment requests and by conducting a background check of the watch seller in question. While sometimes totally fine, cash payment requests should still be regarded with special caution. At the risk of stating the obvious, don't pay cash for an expensive watch you buy from a private seller. Even an in-person deal shouldn't require a watch investor to present himself to a stranger with thousands of dollars on his person.

In the year 2021, massive cash handovers are the primary domain of thieves and drug dealers, not watch investors. Rather stick to checks, escrow accounts, credit cards, and bank wires. Bank wire or escrow payments for high-end watches present both the most convenient option and a better chance to fact-check one's counterparty. Always ensure that the given bank, address, and owner name for the seller's account corresponds to the seller's region, country, and identity. If a watch seller of a given name purportedly in Canada specifies a bank in Turkey with a different account name, think at least twice and ask hard questions.

Misrepresentation serves as a legal catch-all term for hazards arising from dealing with sellers, although it primarily refers to online and distance sellers. It can take all kinds of forms and typically comprises inaccurate descriptions of the external or cosmetic condition (most common), photoshopping or editing pictures, inaccurate function condition, wrong information on age/ownership documentation and, last but not least, genuineness of all parts. In certain cases, a watch collector may detect misrepresentation in photos or descriptions as the first clue that something is amiss. Watch investors should be on alert for one hazard indicating another more often than not. Unlike outright replica scams, like the infamous and widely discussed Horology House Daytona scam in early 2020, misrepresentation can even involve reputable dealers and by its very nature does not necessarily involve the seller's intention. And this is a crucial point to understand for the novice watch investor: even a reputable seller might fall victim to negligence from time to time in this business, which is why vigilance as a buyer is the only real way to avoid potentially large-scale losses.

With these guidelines you can already significantly reduce the risk of falling victim to misrepresentation of some sort. The most important rule remains: buy only what you know. You should only buy references where you did the necessary due diligence, i.e. the ones that you fully understand. Warren Buffett's approach to stock picking works also for watches. Any watch investor has to build the relevant knowledge not only to identify bargains but also to guard against incompetent sellers, inaccurate descriptions, and of course fraudulent, unscrupulous rip-off attempts.

Most importantly, written descriptions of the cosmetic watch condition and documentation must match the photos provided by the seller. Any refusal to provide the investor with such authentication material is a clear warning sign and might be a prelude to a misrepresentation scenario. A hard reality check before pulling the trigger on a deal that is too good to be true is always crucial. And in order to leave emotion during this phase of purchase process truly out of play, the necessary expert knowledge has to be gained in advance. There is no shortcut to this approach or to the need to educate oneself. The threat posed by misrepresentation and outright counterfeits can only be minimized by prior self-education and diligence. It is crucial for you, the aspiring watch investor, not to want too much too early in order to guarantee a long and successful watch investment "career".

Five Steps To Avoid Watch Disasters

I. Go offline if you can. The internet had changed the watch world already, and the global pandemic made it even more digital. Still, whenever possible, I advise to ultimately close the deal offline and inspect the watch in person before your purchase. If the watch is sold within a few hours of radius, schedule a trip to visit some friends, pass by a dealer during business travel or convince your fiancé of the necessity of a weekend getaway. Preferably buy from reputable dealers (such as the ones on our list in Part II)

II. Bring a loupe. If buying (vintage) online, demand numerous, detailed outside photos from all angles and follow our dial examination guide in Part III. Undertake equal diligence of other parts such as the case (especially look for polishing alterations) and bracelet (watch out for irreparable stretch). Watch for any disparity between the photographs and the description provided by the seller and see them as potential warning signs. As mentioned before, high-resolution images of the dial condition are crucial as many brands/models sell primarily based on the strength/crispness of dial condition and originality. Any signs for re-dialing or independent watchmaking might be red flags. Similarly, any physical alterations such as water damage or major scratches on the dial are reason to move on.

III. Confirm in writing. The mechanical operation and functional condition of a watch are virtually impossible to check remotely. Albeit some dealers started to offer videos and VR viewings of their online listings, the power reserve or the chronoscope health cannot be ascertained from home. Here it is important to have some form of written confirmation and/or after-sales guarantee that usually comprises several months and sometimes up to 2 years on the mechanical functional condition of the watch. In case there is a problem with the mechanical condition of the watch such as the chronograph pusher does no longer work correctly, a full-refund for malfunction should be held fixed in writing.

IV. Have a look inside. For vintage pieces always demand photos of the open, exposed movement and look in the highest zoom for any signs of water damage, loose parts or any inauthentic parts. Take a similar approach as for dial examination also for the movement and compare it with pictures of your due diligence resources. If a seller claims to be unable to open the case back (happens more often than you think) be extra skeptical and consider again to pass. If you are hearing this from a dealer – run. Remember also that the often-claimed term waterproof is a temporary condition, not a never-changing feature. Water damage can be a crucial point for dive watches, that have fallen victim to aggressive use or weak water sealing by a less than great watch smith. Repair bills to vintage movements can easily outpace the value of a watch by thousands of dollars, so be careful.

V. Make sure you get what you pay for. Always inspect the additional documentation in form of box and papers if you do decide to pay for it. The paid-for documentation does not just have to be there, it has to be complete. Look for full completeness including all certificates, warranty cards and unique accessories (such as the Rolex COSC tag). Don't pay a premium for a *full set* if you get only an *almost* full set.

Post-Acquisition Phase

Portfolio Construction

The temptation to rush ahead and acquire a series of watches right away is often huge, even more, if you have already set a certain budget aside. However, steady and slow portfolio construction are the preferred way to go. Don't let emotions come in the way and don't push yourself to allocate all the funds you set aside within a short timeframe. You should rather pencil in several months, even years until your portfolio will be sort of complete (although it might like mine remain rather in a state of flux). Focus on *steady* accumulation of rare, high-quality pieces that you fully understand and where you did all the necessary work. Even an extensive, diverse portfolio does not help much if these simple ground rules are broken. You should plan your portfolio development of course, but you also always have to remain open to the element of surprise, when an unexpected opportunity arises, and an incredible investment opportunity presents itself to you.

Market timing can sometimes be crucial in constructing a portfolio, especially for watch models where prices vary much and are subject to larger volatility swings. It is also for this reason that you should not acquire all your portfolio in a certain market phase, e.g. within a short time frame of, say, only a few weeks. While you might encounter a set of excellent investment opportunities especially in times of depression and financial crisis, usually your risk exposure will be tilted significantly when compressing the time frame where you pull the trigger and invest. If an opportunity to do so is simply too good to pass, then you should at least be aware of the then higher skew of your portfolio. Also, have an eye on liquidity. As said before, a good basis for any portfolio is a collection of rather liquid (value) pieces such as pre-Daytona manual wound Rolexes, Gilt-Rolexes or Patek Philippe eternal calendars. Such models give your portfolio the necessary stability. You might also include some contemporary (*growth*) models such as a modern Royal Oak. Over time you can also add more exotic models with less liquidity, but the base liquidity level of your portfolio has already been established.

Storage Logistics

Once you have conducted your first purchases, the question of how your watch portfolio is stored is next. You want to make sure your investments maintain their condition and stay safe. As your portfolio continues to grow the security aspect gains importance. Even though watches are made to last, they require adequate care and protection in order to maintain them in good working condition. Whether you are using a solution at home or external storage for (parts of) your portfolio remains your choice and depends on various individual circumstances. Storage either in a watch winder, the original box or a multi-watch storage box should be a no-brainer to protect your investments from dust and humidity. In case security measures at your home are insufficient, most banks offer safe deposit boxes or private vault facilities where the risk of theft is vastly minimized. Good safe deposit boxes in major cities even offer temperature control to preserve watches better. Such a temperature-controlled safe deposit box or a secure home safe are usually the ideal solutions. Regardless of the option you chose, always be aware to protect your portfolio as best as possible against their biggest enemy: humidity. Moisture is the natural enemy number one of any mechanical timepiece. One easy way to combat the dangerous effects of moisture is to store watches always with silica gel, a technique that many gun owners also use for decades.

Servicing

It is no news that mechanical watches need regular servicing and maintenance. As such the cost of servicing your watch needs to form part of your investment decision. Even for entry-level pieces, it is not uncommon to have a watch service bill surpass $1,000 quite easily, which can cause headaches to investors that are not prepared and did not calculate this part into their investment case. Hence, it is important to always know *before* how easy a watch can be serviced and at what intervals.

From here it is only a short step to get a rough estimate of the running service costs. The frequency of these costs depends also somewhat on whether you actually wear the watch at times or leave it permanently in a safe deposit box. When speaking about servicing I once more want to underline that you should always resist any temptation to restore or clean dials and keep any restoration work to the absolute bare minimum. Movement oiling and servicing are important and keys to preserve the precious heart of your timepiece, but any alterations of its original condition are in 99 percent of all cases a *faux-pas*. Even if there is light rust or minor damage on parts, always make a very careful decision on whether you want to terminally alter the original condition of your watch.

Exit Considerations

At some point, you will want to realize your investment gains. This differentiates you as an investor from a pure collector. For this, you have the same channels available as you had when buying. Unsurprisingly many of the advantages and disadvantages occur vice-versa when you decide to sell a watch. You can sell directly to a private individual, via a marketplace platform, to a trusted dealer (or negotiate for him to sell for a commission) or go via an auction house. The basic rules of supply and demand still apply in the world of watches, particularly in what sells where. According to Phillips star auctioneer Aurel Bacs, for example, *"European collectors prefer a well-pronounced patina to a dial whereas Asian collectors are more perfectionists."* So, be mindful of regional preferences and adjust your sale strategy accordingly. The shares of a listed company are usually tradeable on a handful of stock exchanges. In contrast to the stock market, however, there are hundreds of markets for a particular watch model to be sold. From the local vintage watch dealer in Monaco to the world's big auction houses in London or New York—anything is possible. Why is this so important for the watch investor? As a matter of fact, the same watch can yield vastly different results when sold on various marketplaces. The market for watch investments is so inefficient that it offers the possibility for so-called geo-arbitrage. One tactic for exploiting geo-arbitrage would be to acquire a watch from a private seller in a country where the economy is doing badly due to a recent crisis and selling it later at a large auction house in a booming economy on the other side of the planet (this example is highly theoretical, but you get the point). In the real world, there are certain premium markets where the clientele is willing to pay more: the same watch will most likely yield more if offered from a dealer in Munich than from one based in Moldavia. Should you go for a platform sale, always go the extra mile by describing and photographing your timepieces using lots of details and making the best possible images possible.

Taxes

Like in every other asset class, also the watch investor shall not do his investment strategy and calculations without the tax question. Depending on your own circumstances, your country of residence and the frequency and amount of transactions you conduct, different rules apply. From tax-free gains to light taxation everything is possible, and a detailed analysis would go over the limits of this book. Speculative transactions during the year might be treated differently than capital gains from long-term holdings. In any case, watch investors should have their tax status checked and, if necessary, include taxes in their return consideration and holding strategy.

Case Study: Buying A Neo-Vintage Chronograph

A while ago, Jean-Claude, a good friend of mine and successful investor approached me since he wanted to start investing in watches, particularly in vintage pieces. He was buying contemporary pieces for a while, but never really ventured into the vintage world. In the contemporary space, he invested almost exclusively into Patek Philippe. Also for the vintage world, my friend had a very clear objective: inspired by the legacy of the legendary Ref. 1518 he wanted to buy a vintage Patek perpetual calendar chronograph. This was supposed to be his steppingstone to embark on a journey into the vintage world. When he consulted me to discuss the pros and cons of several models, I could not let him down.

We went together through a range of Patek chronographs such as the typical references 1518, 2499, 3970, 5020, and 5270. We skipped the 1518 for obvious reasons ($$$) and started with the 2499, an incredibly hard-to-get icon watch, limited in good quality supply and financially also already out-of-reach for Jean-Claude's endeavor. Quickly we reached the relatively more affordable successor Ref. 3970—a wonderful reference with very similar characteristics as its big brother but produced from 1986 to 2004 at ca. 10x the volume of a Ref. 2499. Jean-Claude quickly settled on this particular reference. For him, this neo-vintage reference was a clear future icon, set to appreciate similarly to the bigger brother Ref. 2499 (which was getting increasingly rarer and financially out-of-reach for most players in the market). He was happy to trade down on the reference and go for this highly investable model that was getting more and more sought-after by collectors.

Somewhere between 2,400 and 3,600 watches are produced of the 3970. Less than 30 years old, this neo-vintage reference will fall into the true vintage category in a few years. It is powered by a Caliber CH27-70 based on the Lemania 2310 movement, while the predecessor 2499 was equipped with a Valjoux-based movement. The watch sports a modern-looking, well-sized 36mm case and was produced in yellow, white, and rose gold, as well as in platinum. There are three different series of the 3970. The first two series, which are the most valuable, had Feuille (leaf-shaped) hands and baton hour markers. The third series has baton center hands. It's also worth mentioning that there are some with full 18-karat gold screw-down case backs and others with sapphire crystal exhibition case backs. The solid gold case backs are considered more valuable since they were only manufactured for about three years. We established to search for a first or second series in rose gold with Feuille hands, baton hour markers, and a full gold screw-down case back. While screening we came across 3970s ranging from around €60k to twice the price tag. The cheaper ones would usually be a third series model, lack B&P and often had been polished. The ones for €100k+ would be second series models with full documentation. Ultimately, the condition made all the difference and while Jean-Claude was tempted at times, I held him back from buying a few presumed bargains in inferior condition. Together we used the same methodology and similar sources as I do usually. To study the references in more detail we used many of the usual books (mentioned earlier in Part IV), blogs, and even called a Patek Philippe vintage expert in Zurich to crosscheck some of the information we gathered. Both of us scanned the auction market and checked-out the inventory of the go-to watch dealers globally (see Part II). In the process, we noted down how many pieces of the 3970 were sold over the last five years, comparing the sale prices of the yellow gold, rose gold, white gold, and platinum models. We also recorded how many complete sets were sold and determined which geographic locations had the best values to make sure we conduct geo-arbitrage if at all possible. With this extensive price information, we had a fairly good view of what price range would be considered a decent entry point for this investment if the *reference-trade-down-thesis* would hold. This made it easier to systematically monitor the market and after a couple of months, to find an excellent 3970 that matched all these parameters. What a lovely journey that was!

Buying a vintage investment-grade watch, especially at this elevated price range, takes plenty of time and effort, and my friend was very pleased to have conducted a large bulk of the work himself. It's a beautiful watch that will soon become a vintage piece, and if we are right, it will by then probably pick up significantly in value.

The Flipside: Risks of Watch Investing

Welcome to the dark side. To conclude this chapter we will now look briefly at things that can go wrong in watch investing to help you to take precautionary steps. Niche asset class watch investments comprise a completely different set of risk factors compared, for example, to mainstream assets such as stocks or real estate. While some of these factors are immediately apparent to the seasoned investor there is also a whole range of risk factors that are less obvious. These factors include such things the increasingly saturated vintage market, changes in taste, the danger of the increasingly sophisticated fraud and replica industry as well as fads and bubbles.

Transaction Costs & Illiquidity

First of all, the costs of acquiring and selling a watch are significantly higher than selling shares via an online brokerage account. Fees of auction houses and dealer markups can make up a significant percentage of your returns and must be watched carefully. Watch auction houses charge a premium to the buyer as well as often a commission to the seller for their efforts. Dealers usually seek to buy from you at a discount. This implies that frequent buying and selling, as possible for stocks, is not possible with watches and long enough holding periods are needed to successfully amortize and spread the transaction costs over the investment period. This can be an advantage for individual investors, though, who do not want to make watch investing a full-time job and might in fact prefer a lower trade frequency. Many watches are, moreover, subject to an illiquidity discount that might constitute a form of cost itself. Generally speaking watches are more comparable to selling a house than a stock or bar of gold. If you want to achieve *market value,* you might need to wait for the next big auction in the respective area and niche. These auctions are not held continuously, and it is possible that several months of waiting are necessary just to get the theoretical chance of addressing the most suitable set of potential buyers and realizing the true market value of your watch. Even more so, auction houses often will decline requests to sell items when they consider the market not at the right time or the fit with the other products is not given. This might mean that your vintage minute repeater watch will not be presented at Christie's next auction unless you have established connections to the house. This matter is somewhat easier for lower priced (<$100k) watches where many sales are conducted via online channels.

"Auction houses pick their watches one by one, creating a bottleneck in the market. To sell a range of complications, it could take 15 to 18 months."

– Massimo Monti (Lankarani, 2010)

Additional expenses for storage and insurance are lowering net returns that can be achieved in the watch sector. The costs of this depend largely on whether the purchase has been made as a pure investment. For such cases storage solutions such as a bank deposit box are cost effective and not much higher than brokerage fees on your stock portfolio.

Changing Tastes

This one is an obvious point. If we assume relatively constant supply by top watchmakers, returns of watch investments ultimately depend on expectations of future demand. However, demand for a certain watch type can be hard to predict as tastes tend to change over time. For example, the Rattrapante complication was vastly out-of-fashion in the 1970s while it is today achieving record results at auctions and is in high demand among watch investors. When trying to observe historical patterns, it is crucial to watch for survivorship bias in such analyses. Only God knows what the superstar watches over the next century will be, especially when we are currently seeing one of the biggest changes in the watchmaking world: the second wave of electrification. Today, Apple is already the biggest "watchmaker" and the euphoria for smartwatches outpaces the watch industry's worst nightmares by far. This might have consequences in future that we cannot yet assess, even if the high-end market seems less open to attack than the lower-end market.

Changes in Wealth Pattern

Another possible risk is global wealth distribution, which can have significant long-term impacts on the demand for certain watch models and their prices. Similarly to the art world, where the Japanese boom in the 1980s caused a strong price increase for artists' works favored by Japanese collectors, a similar boom is possible with the emergence of China and other developing countries that are developing a taste for certain watch manufacturers and models. Some academics say, that the strong connection between wealth and the demand and hunger for luxury watches also can be seen as a possible reason why collectibles such as watches have a certain correlation to equities at times, thus weakening the rationale for investing in watches purely out of diversification. It has to be mentioned, however, that such a correlation usually occurs with a significant lag, which again favors the diversification argument in the short-to-mid-term (Dimson & Spaenjers, 2014).

Speculative Sentiment

As the popularity and premium retail prices of certain contemporary watches such as the Rolex Ref. 126610LV aka Starbucks shows, sentiment does play a massive role and the borders between investing and speculation are oftentimes somewhat blurred in the watch investing world. This is no surprise given the difficulty and inefficiency with which price information is distributed in the watch world. Throw in the emotional or passion component of a purchase and the impossibility to short-sell potential fads and bubbles and you won't be surprised that sentiment is of high importance in the watch market.

Maturing Market

As with every market that is at the beginning of its time, it is getting increasingly harder for investors to make money as the market becomes more mature and the field of fellow investors is getting more competitive. This is exactly the case for the watch market. Though it was possible 15 years ago to find incredible bargain watches at local flea markets (like I did in the early 2000s), the constantly improving availability of price

177

information through the internet and auction websites makes this increasingly less likely as interest in vintage watches keeps growing. However, not all hope is gone. Yes, there is always that tiny little remote possibility of coming across an important and valuable timepiece in a thrift shop. Only a few years back, a modified Breitling Top Time fetched a record price of $160k as it was the model worn by James Bond while filming *Thunderball* on the remote islands of Exuma in the Bahamas. The watch was allegedly discovered at a car boot sale.

Imperfect Substitutes
One common share of a listed S&P 500 company is a perfect substitute for another one. However, a 1974 Rolex COMEX Sea-dweller offered in an auction by Sotheby's is not a perfect substitute of the same reference Rolex offered by a private individual. The differences between the watches can be so different that one model can command more than 10x the price of the other. The unique characteristics determine the return potential in the world of watches.

Replicas and Frauds
While scams can be found in the real estate or financial markets, investors in watches need to be particularly careful. The increasingly sophisticated vintage watch replica market is of highest concern, not only because it might trick you into buying a franken-watch but because it can also damage the long-term market dynamics if investors start to shy away from this market segment. Another related issue concerns the purchase of watches without any certificate of ownership—i.e. potentially stolen watches. Buying a stolen or frankened watch from unscrupulous or uninformed dealers is a real risk for investors.

Reverse Buyers
A so-called reverse buyer is another potential risk factor for watch investors. This term is used when a brand serves both as supplier and as auction buyer. While this might not make immediate sense, this situation is exactly the case in the Patek Philippe auction market. The Stern family, which controls Patek Philippe, represents one of the most prominent and

active buyers in the Patek Phillippe auction market. Imagine now what could happen if Mr. Stern, president of Patek Philippe, decided to increase or vary production of a certain model. His actions alone would have certainly the power to move whole vintage market segments.

Market Makers

Size matters not only on the wrist in the watch-investing world. Investors of significant size can act as market makers. If a large-scale watch investor such as a billionaire collector or watch investment fund is large enough, it might in theory move the market alone. If, for example, a large-scale investor determines a certain watch is undervalued, he can buy many or all still available pieces often in one go, thereby driving prices up. Such watch investment funds do appear and disappear every now and then. The most important one is certainly Alfredo Paramico's Precious Time Fund that started in the early 2010s.

Opaqueness of the Market

Investing in watches means operating in a still somewhat opaque market where not all watches are sold in auctions, but the majority—especially in the not ultra-high-end range—is sold from one person to another. These private exchanges are only to a certain extend traceable and not based on hard data. The *taste* of the individuals transacting, and their individual circumstances are often the key drivers behind this market segment, making it increasingly opaque. Unfortunately, most of these sub-markets are also not transparent in terms of pricing. So-called front-running, i.e. driving the auction price up by agreed bids, has become the order of the day. This regularly leads to hidden overvaluations because, unlike with stocks or bonds, there is no real transaction behind a bid as the goods are only available once—at the moment of the auction. It is therefore easy for a group of bidders to come to an agreement and raise the price without any obligation to buy.

Part IV – Chapter Summary:

- The process of buying a (classic) watch can generally be divided into two phases: the pre-acquisition phase, which consists of *knowledge building, screening, due diligence* and *valuation*, as well as the post-acquisition phase, which consists of *storage* and *exit*
- Hand in hand with the due diligence phase goes the determination of the fair value of a watch, i.e. the appropriate price you should pay as an investment
- Be careful and pay attention to red flags to avoid scams, replicas, frankens and other rip-offs. Franken watches are hard to be spotted and scammers always reinvent themselves with new fraudulent schemes. And even if genuine, as with any other investment, investing in watches is not free from *normal* risks ranging from transaction costs to speculative sentiment

Part V: Getting Started

The $10,000 Question

S o, the burning question is now: how do you get started with building our very own investment-grade watch portfolio in order to protect your wealth better from a perfect storm in the global financial system and potentially rising inflation after the global pandemic? I strongly assume that after making it until this stage of the book, you cannot wait to get your hands dirty and desperately want to start building knowledge about watch references. In short, you want to start putting money to play. Purchasing an overlooked *value* reference in pristine condition and with a proven auction history like the Patek Ref. 3790 of Jean-Claude might seem like a great way to start. The practical problem is that this would set you back already ten thousands of dollars. So how to get started in an investment

181

discipline where the assets can require easily six-figure sums to get engaged? What if you don't have $100k spare cash lying around that waits to be invested? Contrary to the stock market you cannot simply purchase a certain share of a watch. While there come and go apps and concepts that allow buying partial ownership stakes in watches and artworks, there are no Paul Newman Daytona B-shares like for a Berkshire Hathaway stock. You have to buy the entire watch. The burning question is, therefore: how to start *on a budget?*

Here's the good news: it is possible to start watch investing with the same amount that you would have started an average stock market portfolio with (at a few years back in the pre-Robinhood era where transaction costs in stocks required a certain minimum account size to be sensible). We talked a lot about six-to-seven figure record prices at global auctions for the world's rarest Patek Philippe and Rolex models. While these headlines are often at the forefront of our minds, it is simply not true that you can only acquire excellent investment pieces at large scale high-profile auctions in price ranges, hardly attainable and prohibitively expensive for most watch investors. There is a much wider range of absolutely stunning investment pieces sold at local dealers, online or at smaller auctions. These make incredible investments and start already at less than the price of a brand-new Rolex Submariner on the grey market. Not only paying big bucks for the highest quality brands can get you started in watch investing. Hence, let me assure you: success in watch investing does not depend on a seven-figure cash balance, even if record auction results might lead you to think that!

Rather the very opposite is true: the lower the amount of capital invested, the easier it is to find some sort of edge versus other market participants since lower-priced models do not demand the same amount of investor and collector attention. Therefore, you can get an edge over the average collector more easily and make a decent first investment. While there are many ways how to approach your first investment watch, I give you some food for thought in this chapter. I will give you a rough orientation point on how to get started. Obviously, in reality, every investor starts differently depending on their individual circumstances, so this is not a step-by-step guide but simply a framework on how to think about watches at an entry-level price point. Is $10k enough to get started? Absolutely. Can you start with even less capital? Probably, but then you won't have a portfolio and need to focus on one, or maybe two watches. So the $10k question is: what watches should you be buying?

Rolex, Patek, Gruen?

"Personally, I sometimes prefer a Longines chronograph to a Patek Philippe chronograph, depending on the condition and the model. You can find rare, excellently well-made watches that are likely to gain further value at Mido, Omega, or Audemars Piguet."

– Alfredo Paramico (Maillard, 2017)

When it comes to investment-grade timepieces you know that the two super brands Rolex and Patek Philippe are monopolizing the top auction rankings. These two are trailed by the rest of the watch brand crowd, with large distances between them. While this is certainly true for the highest-end spectrum of the watch investing world, it is, however, only part of the story. When you start researching and investing in watches you will encounter an amazing fact: the brand matters less than you think in the *entry-level* price segment. What?! Yes, you heard it right. I contradict myself. And let me explain why: with a limited budget, certain compromises have to be made. These compromises shall certainly not be on condition and only partially on rarity. If we do have to make trade-offs, it can be the brand in the entry-level vintage segment. Don't get me wrong: value dynamics such as limited supply, degree of complication, or provenance are equally important for lower-priced, entry-level timepieces. Of course, the higher the brand in the pyramid hierarchy we saw in Part III, the better. The point I want to make is that it is completely fine to acquire a rather special $3k Gruen or Universal Genève, that is in pristine condition and virtually ticks all the boxes. In this price range, it is more important to keep transaction costs low and minimize potential service costs by buying serviced pieces in excellent condition. But sure, if you consider spending a significantly higher amount right away from the start, then a brand such as Rolex or Patek Philippe simply provides a higher moat safeguarding your investment as well as more favorable price momentum. As so often in life, it's all a matter of budget in the end.

Three Investment Approaches

There are many ways to start watch investing and there is no holy grail approach on which route to take. I outline here three strategies that are in my view appropriate for novice investors with a mid-to-long-term investment horizon. Rather than clearly leaning into one camp, it might work best for you to combine them. The watch market is changing constantly, and this is no specific investment advice, but simply illustrating some potential routes:

Strategy 1: Tier-2 Icons

The first strategy focuses on iconic pieces of Tier-2 brands. A great strategy that allows you to be at the forefront of a brand's lineup and invest in their most iconic pieces, without completely breaking the bank because you are going straight for Patek Philippe or Audemars Piguet. A striking example would the Omega Speedmaster Professional line.

Such icons offer a pay-off similar to a long-dated zero-coupon bond, where you benefit from the price appreciation in a very stable high-quality asset. Timepieces with great underlying momentum like the Tudor Submariner can offer an equally attractive outlook. The liquidity of these Tier-2 icons is usually decent, and the price volatility is on the lower end.

Strategy 2: Reference Trade-Down

The second strategy that works well in constructing an entry-level watch investment portfolio is *trading down* on the reference while sticking with a top-tier brand. This is an investment approach that worked very well in the past and will likely do so in future as the prime models and flagship references get increasingly rarer and quickly out of reach for many collectors and investors. This strategy means you focus on lesser-known, less in-demand models within a certain brand family. It allows you to profit from a brands heritage, and, if you pick the right reference you might end up *tomorrow* with a model of an almost equal rarity as the flagship timepiece everybody is talking about *right now*. Significant value appreciation and huge returns are not unusual for this strategy. More often than not, current taste for size or case materials are the reasons why some models are available for a significant discount to the flagship models that are in highest demand. And also in the watch world demand comes and goes in waves. Especially with a longer investment horizon, this means that you can have a significant lever as long as you have the stamina to hold on until taste changes. There is a fine line to walk, but history has shown, that if you focus in particular on references that are very closely related to the flagship references, there is often a high chance for a disproportionate gain from buying what stands currently in the shadow of its big brother. This does not mean you should necessarily buy a yellow gold quartz Nautilus, but rather consider more nuanced moves.

A great example are the mid-sized vintage Royal Oaks from Audemars Piguet (e.g. the Ref. 14790ST in our sample checklist). Compared to other models within the family, these are trading at a significant discount, largely because they are somewhat smaller than the original Jumbo. The 14790ST measures only 36mm but wears like 39mm due to its lugs. The ideal men's watch size for such a classic, understated and dressy timepiece. At the time of writing, mid-sized steel versions can be had for slightly under $12,000. However, while it never will be as much en vogue or hyped as the one and only, classic Jumbo version, prices for a Royal Oak Jumbo Ref. 5402 have risen and risen over the last decade and people will likely start looking more and more at alternatives that have the same core characteristics as the classic version.

All in all, it is fair to assume as underlying investment thesis for the Ref. 14790ST that the current discount to the Ref. 5402 of approximately 60-70 percent will never evaporate fully but reduce significantly over the next years (to say 25 percent) as this already relatively rare watch becomes rarer and the value drivers brand, condition, and provenance re-gain importance over current size and fashion trends. And don't forget: even if the discount stays as wide as it is, your investment should still appreciate in line with the big brother!

Another great entry level investment case where you trade-down on the reference are neo-vintage Rolex Explorer IIs (Ref. 16570). With prices of other neo-vintage sports Rolexes reaching nose bleeding altitudes, the Explorer II is still a real bargain. Until recently they were available at bargain prices around $5k. The current taste prefers the sportier diving and GMT lines of Rolex and the neo-vintage Explorer IIs can be a real steal. If you want to go bigger there is also the contemporary Rolex Explorer II Ref. 216570, the 42mm model that is shockingly neglected by the collector community and a clear "sleeper" in the shadow its, more famous Rolex brothers. The contemporary Explorer II does hardly wear larger than the new, updated 41mm Submariner and at the time of this writing it is still trading at discount to its MSRP. What happens if Rolex would decide to discontinue this model is your guess. But one thing is sure. The pandemic-inspired outdoor boom made *adventure* more en vogue than ever before. Both of these Rolex models are based on a watch that had originally been designed for cave explorers. Can it be more adventurous?

Strategy 3: Out-of-Favor Manufacturers
The third strategy that can be used to put together an entry-level portfolio is somewhat different from the first two as it involves higher risk. Rather than going for the tier-1 brands, you would focus in this strategy on *neglected manufacturers* seeking to acquire models from overlooked out-of-favor brands that are either on the verge of being *re-discovered* or *resurrected* or simply temporarily out-of-fashion. Striking examples of previously resurrected brands include vintage Panerais or Blancpains before their major revival through the Swatch Group.

In practice, this strategy involves on the one hand investing in brands that ceased to exist (such as Cairelli or Universal Genève) and on the other hand in brands (or parts of their historical line-up) that are at the moment out-of- favor. Examples for the latter would be early Breitling offerings from the 1940-50s or many of the first Longines chronographs. These are nowadays available for great value if you search properly. Remember that it is always smarter to buy the best example of a less-expensive watch than the worst example of a more-expensive watch. By focusing on lesser-known brands first, you might not own that portfolio of iconic dream Rolex watches right away but will slowly progress towards it.

Putting Theory into Practice

When deciding which of the three strategies to focus on, let some time pass before narrowing down which style suits your personality best. I suggest you pick up a couple of auction catalogues, flip through them and do some initial research on references and brands that you find intellectually fascinating (aside from the obvious candidates you are probably thinking of already), and you should soon have a better feeling in which of the strategies you are more willing to invest your time and capital in. Understand just exactly what it is that appeals to you in a certain category of watches, ideally aside from the pure financial investment parameters. Is it the romance of a particular brand? Does your pulse quicken at the name of legendary models, say, early vintage Longines watches? If so, I would start doing the homework, assess potential pitfalls and try to become a specialist by speaking to other investors in this brand and model range. You should not necessarily focus on the massive bargain of the century for your first watch investment. If you overpay 5 to 10 percent that's fine. If you get a small discount to market value, incredible! In the beginning, you simply must avoid large blunders and get comfortable with the whole investment process.

Watch investing is a marathon, not a sprint and it is more important to avoid huge errors than hitting a home run right at the beginning of your watch investing career.

If you did complete the initial homework and still cannot decide on your preferred approach, a so-called barbell approach might work for you. Here you would structure a portfolio with a core of relatively safe investments with lower return potential (e.g. tier-2 icons) which are enriched by some more exotic, higher risk-reward satellite investments (e.g. an out-of-favor manufacturer). In the middle of this risk-reward spectrum, there is virtually nothing, like a barbell.

In reality, there are much more possible approaches to investing your hard-earned cash than I could ever suggest, but in my view, it is advisable to rather start conservatively and concentrated. This means that for the start, investing in a classic Rolex Sport Model is my preferred advice over some moon-shot bets. You should be able to end up e.g. with one Rolex Explorer II in good condition and one vintage dress watch (e.g. the Genta-designed Universal Genève Polerouter). It would only be logical if Rolex would finally introduce an updated version of Explorer II in 2021/22, which could then have a positive effect on prices not only for the vintage models (Ref. 1655) but most likely also on the neo-vintage re-editions.

In case there is enough budget left a look at vintage Cartiers could be an option too. The Tank is the definitive straight-sided watch design and many vintage and neo-vintage models such as the Basculante Ref. 2405 are an incredible value and a bargain in light of their limited production runs. And while they are unlikely to go through the roof in terms of prices, they should continue appreciating steadily and could complement your starting portfolio. A different route would be to bet on military provenance and invest in one of the still heavily undervalued Tier-2 military pieces. This market subsegment emerged from the popularity of the Rolex MilSub watches. Especially the "Dirty Dozen" (a series of watches commissioned by the UK military in 1945) offers an attractive value proposition. Also the Heuer and Leonidas Bundeswehr pilot flyback Chronos are great undervalued options in this segment that make nice portfolio additions. With only a few of these picks, you then have in theory already a small watch *portfolio*. Did we surpass the mentioned $10k? Possibly. But I still insist an (at least) three-watch portfolio is possible in this budget if you try hard enough.

No matter how you ultimately end up structuring your very own watch investment portfolio, you might want to make sure to always strike a nice balance. Betting only on underdogs is not recommendable, but also betting only on already highly sought-after timepieces will not offer great risk-reward. As mentioned before, assuming you did your homework, buy from a reputed dealer or get external advice. I do suggest for most pieces (especially entry-level ones) to buy without box and papers, especially if the initial budget is tight. Without box and papers you may buy each watch around 10-20 percent cheaper, while the overall relative value development will hardly be impacted. The 10-20 percent you save, you can invest in another vintage chronograph or two superior alternatives in better condition, that protect you at the same time from losses through the *disappearing premium*, as explained before in Part III. Over time you can expand your investment portfolio diligently.

Everybody starts small, but this is already an amazing start.

For your starting portfolio, you will probably still be covered by your household insurance and don't necessarily need a safety deposit box at a bank. However, be aware that many insurances have special rules, e.g. for the inclusion of gold watches. Hence you should always check that in advance.

Part V – Chapter Summary:

- Successfully investing in watches does not depend on a certain budget. You can start with the same dollar amount that you would have started an average stock market portfolio with (a few years back)
- The lower the amount of capital invested, the easier it is to find an edge since lower-priced models often do not demand the same amount of investor and collector attention
- Investors can use three strategies to start an entry-level portfolio: the first strategy (Tier-2 Icons) focuses on iconic pieces of second tier brands. Another strategy (Reference Trade-Down) is to trade down on the reference while sticking with a top-tier brand. A third strategy (Out-of-Favor Manufacturers) seeks to acquire models from overlooked brands that are either on the verge of being re-discovered, resurrected or temporarily out-of-fashion

Final Words & Golden Rules

Final Secret

"Look, you can lose your ass off on this stuff. They can be an investment, but this is a secondary thing and should never be the primary reason for buying."

– Eric Ku (A Collected Man, 2021)

By no means it is easy making money with watches. The views and strategies outlined in this book are based on a range of uncertain factors and success is far from guaranteed. The value of an investment-grade watch cannot always be enforced in the market. For this reason, all of the pitfalls and risks described should be taken seriously into account when planning an investment in any watch. Skepticism and a certain degree of paranoia are traits that you have to develop as a successful watch investor if you don't want to overpay and make huge blunders. In contrast to liquid securities like stocks, where the future earnings power of a corporation is traded, the watch market usually only sees the present and is subject to a large degree of inefficiency. Like the stock market, it can be subject to bubbles at times. You have to be careful as this obviously may not play in your favor. Moreover, market prices are merely a snapshot in which sentiment and mood play a greater role than rational aspects at times. This is also why the market prefers to stick with the eternal icons over long periods of time and has shown difficulty in rapidly attributing value to other models. And it is also the reason why the most sought-after brands, won't change dramatically overnight or anytime soon. Every change occurs gradually and slowly. Just like we have the 10 biggest impressionist painters or the 10 greatest car manufacturers, in watches you have many great names with an incredibly rich history. This does not change by tomorrow. So, yes in the year 2030 you will still have Patek Philippe and Rolex up there, setting auction records. But do have other brands such as Audemars Piguet, F.P. Journe or Tudor the potential to catch up in this regard? Absolutely. So much to scare you. But one thing is also clear: investments in watches can be extremely successful when done with passion. Done thoroughly and with a sound, investment process, it is not only unlikely to lose money with watch investments, but you are very likely to pocket nice returns over time. The final secret is in the end—as with most investments—*a bit of luck*. Because even if the probabilities work for you, things can always turn out differently. At last, bear in mind that this book does only scratch the surface of the vintage world and is only a primer. I leave you now with my *Golden Rules of Watch Investing* as a sort of a best-of, but you still have to dive deep into specific references and nurture your knowledge via dedicated due diligence resources and books in order to be successful in this field.

But for now, happy hunting!

12 Golden Rules of Watch Investing

1. **No compromises on condition** – rather buy the best example of the less expensive watch than the worst example of a more expensive watch. Never compromise and stay disciplined when it comes to *condition*. It is the paramount driver of value

2. **Buy the seller first, then the watch** – if a deal seems too good to be true, it probably is – be aware of counterfeits (paranoia is not always a bad thing)

3. **Study, study and study** – do the homework, ask questions and seek independent verification if possible/reasonable. The more watches you review and study the sharper your eye will become. You will be able to invest more confidently and obtain more joy – e.g. from placing a winning bid—if you did your homework

4. **Stay open-minded** – rather than screening only for a particular reference, always have an eye for pieces that stand out due to their condition

5. **Diversify accordingly** – a watch *collection* might not be defined by a certain number, but a *portfolio* should be properly diversified across a couple of timepieces. Three is a good start, more is better

6. **Don't fall victim to hypes** – every year there are new fads and hypes. Think long-term and don't let bubbles and fads influence you. Significant softening on hype pieces always comes when you expect it the least

7. **Don't be afraid to push the button** – you can learn about passion assets by studying them, but you'll know infinitely more once you own them

8. **Get supporting documentation whenever possible** – often it will be lost or destroyed years ago, but if available it can add significant value

9. **Always keep learning** – stop by the watch museums on your business trips to Switzerland, download auction catalogues on your iPad for long-haul flights, meet other collectors and investors whenever possible, etc.

10. **Don't forget to have fun** – emotions and adrenaline during the buying process are a wonderful thing. Making a great investment is a satisfying moment that you should enjoy to its fullest

11. **On the edge, follow your heart** – if in doubt it's better to buy what you would also like even if the price would (temporarily) correct a lot

12. **Take small steps** – Be humble, not too competitive. It's OK to make mistakes but learn from them. Patience is paramount to building your portfolio

198

Resources

A Collected Man. 2020. *Interview: Dr Helmut Crott.* [online] Available at: <https://www.acollectedman.com/blogs/journal/interview-dr-helmut-crott> [Accessed 19 April 2020].

A Collected Man. 2019. *Interview: Anish Bhatt.* [online] Available at: <https://www.acollectedman.com/blogs/journal > [Accessed 2 May 2020].

A Collected Man. 2021. *Interview: Eric Ku.* [online] Available at: <https://www.acollectedman.com/blogs/journal/interview-eric-ku> [Accessed 9 March 2021].

Andhora.com. 2018. *Blog Relojes Vintage — Andhora.Com.* [online] Available at: <https://www.andhora.com/blog/2018/5/28 > [Accessed 26 April 2020].

Barber, T., 2020. *How Phillips' James Marks Has Shaken Up The Watch Auction World.* [online] Spear's Magazine. Available at: <https://www.spearswms.com/how-phillips-james-marks-has-shaken-up-the-watch-auction-world/> [Accessed 12 April 2020].

Bhasin, K., 2018. *The Small Dealers Shaping The Vintage Watch Business.* [online] Bloomberg Businessweek. Available at: <https://www.bloomberg.com/news/features/2018-10-25/the-small-dealers-shaping-the-vintage-watch-business> [Accessed 26 April 2020].

Christie's. 2019. *The Watch Investor: Rolex Submariner, Daytona And Explorer II / Christie's.* [online] Available at: <https://www.christies.com/features/Watch-investor-Rolex-Submariner-Daytona-and-Explorer-II-9807-1.aspx> [Accessed 20 June 2020].

Credit Suisse Research Institute. 2020. *Collectibles: An integral part of wealth.* Available at: < https://www.credit-suisse.com/sg/en/entrepreneurs/global-network/collectibles-report.html> [Accessed 2 January 2021].

De Griff, J., 2019. *Interview: Virginie Liatard-Roessli Watch Specialist.* [online] ATELIER DE GRIFF. Available at: <https://atelierdegriff.com/2019/06/11/interview-virginie-liatard-roessli-watch-specialist-at-phillips-in-association-with-bacs-russo/> [Accessed 18 April 2020].

Dimson, E. and Spaenjers, C., 2014. Investing in Emotional Assets. Financial Analysts Journal, 70(2), pp.20-25.

Easthope, A., 2019. *The Art Of Collecting With Phillips' Watch Expert James Marks.* [online] Classicdriver.com. Available at: <https://www.classicdriver.com/en/article/watches/art-collecting-phillips-watch-expert-james-marks> [Accessed 13 April 2020].

Elite Advisors. 2011. *Precious Time Fund Information.* Available at: < http://rolexpassionreport.com/Rolex.pdf> [Accessed 20 June 2020].

Hashtag Legend. 2016. *Horological Auctioneer Aurel Bacs Talks Independents And The Future Of Watches — Hashtag Legend.* [online] Available at: <https://hashtaglegend.com/style/horological-auctioneer-aurel-bacs-talks-independents-and-future-watches/> [Accessed 18 April 2020].

Investopedia. 2020. *Investopedia.* [online] Available at: <https://www.investopedia.com/terms/i/investment.asp> [Accessed 13 April 2020].

Investopedia. 2020. *Investopedia.* [online] Available at: <https://www.investopedia.com/terms/s/speculation.asp> [Accessed 13 April 2020].

Knight Frank. 2018. *Knight Frank Luxury Report 2018.* [online] Available at: <https://www.knightfrank.com/wealthreport/2018/luxury-spending/luxury-investment-index-2018> [Accessed 9 March 2021].

Knight Frank. 2021. *Knight Frank Investment Index 2020.* [online] Available at: < https://www.knightfrank.com/wealthreport/article/2020-03-03-the-luxury-investment-index-2020-discover-the-worlds-mostcoveted-items> [Accessed 9 March 2021].

Lane, S., 2017. *Buying A New Watch? Don't Even Think About Investment Value.* [online] Time and Tide Watches. Available at: <https://timeandtidewatches.com/opinion-buying-a-new-watch-dont-even-think-about-investment-value/> [Accessed 19 April 2020].

Lankarani, N., 2010. *High-End Watches As An Investment Strategy.* [online] NYT. Available at: <https://www.nytimes.com/2010/03/18/fashion/18iht-acawauction.html> [Accessed 18 April 2020].

Maillard, S., 2017. *Luxury Watch Collector Alfredo Paramico: "There's No Vintage Bubble".* [online] Luxury Society. Available at: <https://www.luxurysociety.com/en/articles/2017/11/theres-no-vintage-bubble/> [Accessed 25 April 2020].

Morgan Stanley. 2019. *Passion Assets: Investing In Art | Morgan Stanley.* [online] Available at: <https://www.morganstanley.com/what-we-do/wealth-management/private-wealth-management/investing-in-art> [Accessed 13 April 2020].

Piters, N., 2019. *Tourbillons To Tachymeters: The Investment-Worthy Details Behind Classic Watches.* [online] The RealReal. Available at: <https://realstyle.therealreal.com/tourbillons-investment-watches-complications-rolex/> [Accessed 2 May 2020].

Private Air, 2015. *Alfredo Paramico Collecting Time.* Available at: < https://world-words.com/wp-content/uploads/2015/01/Alfredo-Paramico.pdf> [Accessed 9 March 2021].

Tan, S., 2016. *Vintage Chronographs In Demand At Auctions.* [online] The Business Times. Available at: <https://www.businesstimes.com.sg/hub/the-business-of-time-2016/vintage-chronographs-in-demand-at-auctions> [Accessed 13 April 2020].

Wolf, C., 2020. *Somehow, The Vintage Watch Market Is Thriving.* [online] GQ. Available at: <https://www.gq.com/story/vintage-watch-market-coronavirus> [Accessed 18 April 2020].

You Exec. 2020. *Principles by Ray Dalio — You Exec.* [online] You Exec. Available at: <https://youexec.com/book-summaries/principles-by-ray-dalio> [Accessed 9 March 2020].

Printed in Great Britain
by Amazon